DIPLOMATIC DISPUTE:

U.S. Conflict with Iran, Japan, and Mexico

HARVARD STUDIES
IN INTERNATIONAL AFFAIRS
Number 39

DIPLOMATIC DISPUTE:

U.S. Conflict with Iran, Japan, and Mexico

by Robert L. Paarlberg, Editor

Eul Y. Park

Donald L. Wyman

Foreword by Robert O. Keohane
and Joseph S. Nye, Jr.

Published by the
Center for International Affairs
Harvard University

Harvard University
Center for International Affairs

Executive Committee

Created in 1958, the Center for International Affairs fosters advanced study of basic world problems by scholars from various disciplines and senior officials from many countries. The research of the Center focuses on economic, social, and political development; the management of force in the modern world; the problems and relations of advanced industrial societies; transnational processes and international order; and technology and international affairs.

The Harvard Studies in International Affairs, which are listed at the back of this book, may be ordered from the Publications Office, Center for International Affairs, 1737 Cambridge St., Cambridge, Mass. 02138, at the prices indicated. Recent books written under the auspices of the Center, listed on the last pages, may be obtained from bookstores or ordered directly from the publishers.

About the Authors_____

Robert L. Paarlberg is an Assistant Professor of Political Science at Wellesley College and a Research Fellow at the Harvard University Center for International Affairs. He received his Ph.D. from Harvard in 1975, and has continued his primary interest in political relations between rich and poor countries. His research has appeared in, among others, *Foreign Affairs, Foreign Policy, and International Organization.*

Eul Y. Park, currently at the Korea Development Institute, Seoul, received his Ph.D. in political economy at Harvard University in 1975, having previously completed an M.A. in East Asian Studies. Dr. Park has held research appointments at the Harvard Center for International Affairs and at the Brookings Institution, Washington, D.C. His research interests lie in the area of international economic relations.

Donald L. Wyman is a Graduate Student Associate of the Center for International Affairs and a Ph.D. candidate in the Department of History at Harvard University. He has also been a consultant to the Commission for the Organization of the Government for the Conduct of Foreign Policy. His research has concerned U.S.-Latin American political and economic relations, Latin American history, and U.S. foreign policy.

CONTENTS

In our recent study, (*Power and Interdependence*, Boston, 1977), we attempted to explore the extent and significance of those modern international political conditions that we have labeled "complex interdependence." Our attention was drawn particularly to the United States-Canada relationship, where the conditions of complex interdependence—multiple channels of contact, multiple issues, and minor role of military force—seemed to be closely approximated. We deliberately chose this atypical case, since it would allow us to determine whether, at least in this instance, the politics of complex interdependence were significantly different from classical international politics as portrayed by realist authors. We found that Canada was quite successful in its postwar dealings with the United States, and we attributed this in part to the effects of complex interdependence.

We were cautious about generalizing from the United States-Canada relationship, and planned in our early research design to carry out comparable studies of American relations with a variety of countries. Limitations on our time as well as our competence forced us to undertake only one such study—of Australia-U.S. relations. We chose this case in order to hold factors of size, political system, and cultural heritage relatively constant, while looking at differences arising from geography and its politico-military implications. We found that the Australia-U.S. relationship differed quite sharply from that between Canada and the United States. On all three dimensions, it was farther from the ideal type of complex interdependence, and Australia did much less well than Canada in achieving its goals in conflicts with the United States.

We characterized our chapter on Australia-U.S. and Canada-U.S. relations as a pilot study rather than as a definitive treatment of the effects of complex interdependence on bilateral relations: we could not validly generalize from only two cases. Thus it is particularly gratifying that Robert L. Paarlberg, Eul Y. Park, and Donald L. Wyman have applied our research design to U.S. relations with Iran, Japan, and Mexico. They ask precisely the same questions and employ the same analytic technique that we developed for our study of U.S. relations with Canada and Australia. Paarlberg, Park, and Wyman experience some difficulty in locating evidence of genuine complex interdependence in U.S. relations with Iran, Japan, and Mexico. They emphasize the role of military force and security concerns in two of these cases, and the structure of a dominant-dependent relationship in the third. Like the Australia-U.S. case, these relationships suggest limitations on the extent to which complex interdependence characterizes world politics.

Paarlberg, Wyman, and Park also found that Mexico, Japan, and Iran often succeeded in securing outcomes favorable to their objectives, despite the superior overall power of the United States. Their success contrasted with Australia's failure, but could not be explained by the political processes of complex interdependence. This finding does not refute our contention that complex interdependence accounted in part for Canada's performance, but it does suggest that complex interdependence is not a necessary condition for the success of weaker partners. Iran, Mexico, and Japan secured advantages from the way in which the United States attempted to maintain its global alliances: the American government found it useful to provide its allies with benefits, and adjust to their desires, when it could do so at relatively low cost to itself.

The findings of the authors should therefore reinforce our skepticism about linear theories of change, as well as about simple conceptions of cause and effect. Complex interdependence is not a universal phenomenon, nor is it the only explanation for the power of the weak. The structure of world military power, and concerns about security, remain important. *Diplomatic Dispute* thus provides qualification as well as elaboration of our findings. It brings new evidence to bear on important issues. We appreciate the care that the authors have shown in their research, and we recommend their work to students of power and interdependence.

Robert O. Keohane
Joseph S. Nye, Jr.

INTRODUCTION:

CONFLICT AND INTERDEPENDENCE

Robert L. Paarlberg

Diplomatic dispute between nations has long been the central concern of world politics. But international conflict must be studied today under new conditions, conditions marked by an unfamiliar sense of global "interdependence." Few doubt that conflict will continue under these new conditions, yet a precise reading of the relationship between conflict and interdependence remains elusive to scholarship. In part, this is because "modernists," who prefer to study interdependence, and "traditionalists," who continue to study conflict, seldom find the means to communicate with each other. Their separate efforts produce little more than judgments of common sense: interdependence does not necessarily *prevent* conflict; some measure of interdependence is *necessary* for conflict to occur; *too much* interdependence can *invite* conflict; and, at the very least, interdependence will *increase the cost* of conflict.

One recent effort to advance the empirical study of conflict and interdependence has been made by Robert O. Keohane and Joseph S. Nye.[1] These two students of interdependence come from the modernist school, but they nonetheless select conflict as the primary object of their comparative study of bilateral relations between allied states. Keohane and Nye concede at the outset that highly interdependent relations among states may be as conflict-ridden as relations of low interdependence, and their analysis incorporates a wide selection of traditional "realist" expectations with regard to the outbreak and settlement of interstate conflicts. But they add an important argument of their own, viz., that under certain modern conditions, conditions which they label "complex interdependence,"[2] patterns of bilateral conflict creation and conflict outcome may develop in an unexpected and non-traditional fashion. Under conditions of "complex interdependence" a weak state may often prevail. Moreover, under such conditions, strong and weak states together will be more likely to observe rules of mutual restraint in resolving disputes, restraint which in turn may permit larger joint gains to be realized. Keohane and Nye offer empirical evidence to support this argument with a comparative study of U.S. conflict relations with Canada and Australia, over an extended time period, 1920-70.[3]

To explore further this notion that conditions of "complex interdependence" will produce unexpected patterns of conflict creation and conflict resolution, Keohane and Nye have suggested an extension of their own study, to include more than Canadian and Australian case evidence. In response to this suggestion, evidence has now been gathered with regard to three additional states: Iran, Japan, and Mexico. Here we review that new evidence with an eye toward checking as well as expanding upon some of the conclusions drawn from the original Canadian and Australian studies.

Iran, Japan, and Mexico

Iran, Japan, and Mexico provide evidence of U.S. conflict with states which vary by geographic proximity, by wealth or by degree of industrial development, and by conditions of alliance, rivalry, military strength, or weakness. Mexico, as a contiguous state, has been selected as an important variant on the Canadian case. Japan has been selected as a non-European democratic industrial case, a U.S. trading partner second only to Canada, a distant Pacific nation like Australia, and a current U.S. ally, but only one generation ago a military adversary. Iran has been selected as a case that differs in crucial respects from both Japan and Mexico. Iran is semi-industrial, non-democratic, non-Pacific, and non-hemispheric. Two decades ago Iran was a weak and impoverished U.S. client, but until recently it was a wealthy and ambitious regional power.

These three new cases are important for their similarities as well as for their differences. During the postwar period, all have been, like Canada and Australia, a part of the American Cold War alliance system. They have all come to associate under U.S. leadership with Western security interests. Similarly, they have all participated within Western spheres of the international economic system. Consequently, in their current dealings with the U.S., they all face the common dilemma of adjusting their alliance policies to an age marked by intensified economic competition within the West and by a somewhat diminished fear of security threats from the East.

But many of these common conditions are unique to the postwar period. To furnish a needed time perspective, U.S. interaction with these three nations will also be described during an earlier "interwar" period, the 1920-39 period in which the U.S. had not yet assumed a posture of global leadership. During this earlier period, a revolutionary government in Mexico challenged established patterns of U.S. economic hegemony in Latin America, an expansionist government in Japan challenged U.S. military interests in Asia and the Pacific, and a xenophobic Iranian government first sought and then rejected closer ties to the U.S. as a means to balance British and Russian hegemony in the Near East. With such historical variation at hand, changing patterns of conflict over time can be reviewed as well as various conflict relations at any one time, or at the present time.

The research presented here does not permit extended generalization beyond the range of U.S. relations with Mexico, Japan, and Iran, or beyond a comparison to U.S. relations with Canada and Australia. Such generalization must await further accumulation of case material treated within the bounds of a similar "comparative conflict" research design. But these three cases alone do afford a newly enlarged view of conflict and interdependence between weak and strong states. And they are enough to suggest two important qualifications to conclusions reached earlier by Keohane and Nye.

First, these three new cases indicate that the specific conditions of "complex interdependence" are not easily satisfied in U.S. foreign relations with most nation states. U.S. relations with Canada do satisfy those conditions, and U.S. relations with some member nations of the European Community may do so as well. But it will be seen that U.S. relations with Iran, with Mexico, and even with Japan, do not. In each of these three new cases, the full dynamic of "complex interdependence," as described by Keohane and Nye, has yet to develop. And, even in the case of Japan, this dynamic may never develop to approximate the Canadian example. U.S. interactions with Japan are diluted by cultural, racial, and geographic distance, and they are still conducted with considerable formality, against a thin backdrop of transnational or transgovernmental activity. Similar restrictions, and others as well, apply to the case of U.S. relations with Iran. And U.S. relations with Mexico, despite some similarities to the Canadian case, fall closer to simple conditions of "dependence" than to fully developed conditions of complex interdependence.

Keohane and Nye were careful not to argue that U.S. relations with Canada are an advance model of U.S. relations with all other nations, least of all those three nations selected for consideration here.[4] But the conspicuous failure of these three new cases to fully satisfy conditions of "complex interdependence" does caution against an indiscriminate appli-

cation of the modernist paradigm to U.S. interaction with a wide variety
of its modern-day allies.

And yet, as a second observation, these three new cases also challenge
a simple traditional expectation that "the strong will prevail." Even
where ideal conditions of complex interdependence were *not* satisfied,
these three "weak" states were able to enjoy some periodic advantage
over the U.S., both in the creation of conflicts which appear on the
diplomatic agenda, and in the substance of conflict resolution.

During the postwar period, Mexico, Japan, and Iran, in different
measure, were all somewhat favored in day-to-day conflict relations
with their much stronger senior ally, the U.S. The source of this unexpected advantage will not be found in modernist conditions of complex
interdependence but rather in a more traditional pattern of sovereign
policy calculations, a U.S. disposition to bear "leadership costs" in the
successful management of its global alliance relations. In the end, this
U.S. disposition will be described as critical to the continued realization
of joint gains in future circumstances of conflict and interdependence.

NOTES

[1]See Robert O. Keohane and Joseph S. Nye, *Power and Interdependence* (Boston: Little, Brown and Company, 1977).

[2]Keohane and Nye define "complex interdependence" in opposition to
a more familiar ideal type of world politics, "realism." The three necessary conditions of realism are that 1) unified nation states are the dominant world actors, that 2) force is an important instrument of national
policy, and that 3) international issues are arranged in hierarchical
fashion, with "high politics" issues such as military security dominating
"low politics" issues such as economic and social affairs. The opposing
ideal type, "complex interdependence," specifies that 1) actors other than
unified nation states will participate directly in world politics, that 2)
force will be an unimportant instrument of policy, and that 3) a clear
hierarchy of issues will not separate "high politics" security concerns
from "low politics" economic and social concerns. See Keohane and Nye,
Power and Interdependence, pp. 24-25.

[3]Keohane and Nye, *Power and Interdependence*, Part III.

[4]Keohane and Nye, *Power and Interdependence*, p. 216.

THE ADVANTAGEOUS ALLIANCE:
U.S.RELATIONS WITH IRAN
1920-1975

Robert L. Paarlberg

THE ADVANTAGEOUS ALLIANCE:
U.S. RELATIONS WITH IRAN
1920-1975

Robert L. Paarlberg

In politics the strong make the rules, presumably to their own advantage. But the weak, if well positioned, may also profit from those rules, so much at the times as to challenge the strong. Well positioned, well endowed, and well allied, Iran has learned to use the rules of the international system in just this fashion.

His Imperial Majesty Mohammed Reza Pahlavi, Shah of Shahs, Light of the Aryans, inherited the throne in 1941. His nation was then weak and impoverished, its commerce dependent upon foreign money, its resources owned by foreign investors, its political system penetrated by foreign agents, and its territory at the very moment occupied by thousands of uninvited British and Russian troops. Even after the war, when the U.S. replaced Great Britain as the dominant foreign power in Iran, the Shah's own throne had to be preserved by the C.I.A. and financed for a decade with hundreds of millions of dollars of U.S. "development aid." Throughout these early years of his reign, the Shah could be lightly dismissed as just another Third World potentate, the convenient creation and the dutiful Cold War client of strategists in Washington, D.C.

Today the Shah no longer depends upon development aid from the U.S., or from anyone else.* He promotes assistance projects of his own, he dreams of a resurrection of the Persian Empire, and has promised that Iran, by the end of the century, will "catch up with Europe." Iran's petroleum is no longer owned by foreign interests, nor is it sold at prices which favor those interests. Iran is now a considerable foreign investor in its own right, and has spent nearly $30 billion since 1972 to replace Great Britain as the dominant military power in the Persian Gulf. The Shah has purchased $10 billion worth of advanced weapons from the U.S. alone, and with these arms he now dares to challenge even the U.S. Undaunted

---

*Editor's Note: This account of U.S. diplomatic conflict with Iran was prepared and completed before the events of the Iranian Revolution of 1978-1979.

by tough talk from Secretary of State Kissinger soon after the fourfold increase in the price of OPEC oil in 1974, the Shah replied, "If you wag your finger at us, we will wag our finger back at you."

The Shah's dream of "buying" his way into advanced standing among the industrial nations of the West has recently run afoul of high import prices, shortages in trained manpower, and insufficient oil revenues. But Iran has nonetheless overcome much of its earlier disadvantage in dealings with stronger external powers. And it has done so within the confines of an international political system "controlled" by those powers. Was oil the only key to the success?

In response to this question, consider the past record of Iran's relations with one stronger external power in particular, the U.S. From this record, and specifically from the record of past diplomatic conflicts with the U.S., we may discover how and when Iran, as a "weak" nation, began to operate a successful diplomacy in its dealings with stronger states.

What follows is a systematic review of diplomatic conflicts between the U.S. and Iran since 1920. In keeping with the research strategy used elsewhere in this volume, changing levels of contact and interaction between the U.S. and Iran will be described, as well as possible changes in the composition of the U.S.-Iranian diplomatic conflict agenda, the changing role of non-state actors (such as multinational corporations) in conflict agenda formation, and changing patterns of conflict settlement, to the advantage of the U.S., Iran, or both nations. It will be seen that Iran and the U.S. did not enjoy mutually advantageous relations during much of this period. A pattern of joint loss in conflict resolution has only belatedly been replaced by a pattern of joint gains. And now in recent years, as levels of interaction and interdependence between the U.S. and Iran have increased, this pattern of joint gain has come under a new strain.

1. Changing Levels of U.S.-Iranian Contact: From Interaction to Interdependence

Modern contact between the U.S. and Iran dates from the founding of an American mission school in northwest Persia in 1829. This early contact, like many to follow, was non-official and "transnational" in character.[1] Until World War I, and even as late as 1941, the U.S. did not maintain intimate diplomatic relations with Iran, as the nation fell within a tightly protected Anglo-Soviet sphere of influence. The treaty of St. Petersburg, signed in 1907 without even the knowledge of the Persian government, had explicitly divided the country into a Russian zone in the north and a British zone in the south, with a narrow buffer zone between.

Hoping to weaken this regime of British and Soviet influence, the Iranian government did what it could after World War I to build contacts with the U.S. In 1921, U.S. oil companies were invited to seek concessions in northern Persia, still a sphere of Soviet control. And in the following year an official American advisory team was invited to Tehran to manage Persian financial affairs. These early efforts proved a failure. The U.S. State Department was reluctant at this stage to challenge Britain and Russia, either by endorsing any single U.S. oil company seeking concessions in Persia, or by nominating an "official" financial adviser.[2] An American adviser, Dr. Arthur C. Millspaugh, was finally dispatched to Persia in 1922, but under formal instruction that he must serve only as a private individual "in the employ of the Persian government." Millspaugh discovered upon his arrival in Tehran that the Persian government was penetrated by Russian and British agents, and that American businessmen could not be attracted to local investment opportunities. Following a violent street attack on a U.S. Consular official in 1924, American oil company representatives gave up their efforts to obtain a concession in Persia.[3] The Millspaugh Mission itself then met increasing political opposition and left Persia three years later, in 1927.

Official U.S. contact with Iran went into decline after the failure of the Millspaugh Mission, reaching a low point in 1936, when the Iranian Legation in Washington was closed for two years. The xenophobic Shah Reza Khan, who had taken to complaining of critical references to his government in the U.S. press, also sent home U.S. missionaries and prevented U.S. newspapers and magazines from entering Iran during this period. Thus, at the outbreak of World War II, official U.S.-Iranian contacts were at a bare minimum. The Near East Division of the State Department carried no Iranian desk officer. The U.S. maintained only a single Consul at Tabriz, and a small official Legation in Tehran, no member of which spoke the Persian language.[4]

Unofficial U.S. contact with Iran also remained at a very low level prior to World War II. Germany was favored by the Shah as a buffer to British influence after the failure of the Millspaugh Mission, and became Iran's largest trading partner between 1935 and 1939. But British financial interests still controlled the powerful Imperial Bank of Iran, which had 14 branches throughout the country, as well as the all-important Anglo-Iranian Oil Company (AIOC), which employed 30,000 people in Iran. Soviet Russia did not maintain such a large commercial presence in Iran, but its 1200-mile common border did allow for compensating varieties of contact. Citizens of Soviet Azerbaijan, some acting in support of the Iranian communist Tudeh party, were able to slip in and out of the country unnoticed.

It was during the 1942-45 period of joint allied military occupation that U.S. contact with Iran first increased to a significant level. British and Soviet troops had entered Iran together in August 1941, under notes of protest against the size of the German colony in Tehran. This invasion ended Iran's reliance upon Germany as a buffering power and renewed official interest in the U.S. On the day of the invasion the Shah sent a message to President Roosevelt requesting that the U.S. "take efficacious and urgent humanitarian steps to put an end to these acts of aggression."[5]

Roosevelt paid only slight heed to this first Iranian request, and the Shah himself was forced to abdicate within a month, leaving the throne to his young son. But during the occupation period Iran continued to seek increasing official ties with the U.S., and the U.S. eventually responded, as its own contribution to the war effort in the Persian corridor grew larger. In 1943, 30,000 U.S. Army troops entered Iran to expedite transport of Lend-Lease supplies to Russia along the Trans-Iranian railroad. In the same year the U.S. upgraded its Legation in Iran to a full Embassy, signed a new bilateral trade agreement, and then sponsored the Tehran Declaration, which offered Iran a guarantee of sovereignty and economic assistance after the war. The U.S. also sent five separate advisory missions to Tehran, to assist not just in financial administration, but also in military reorganization, police training, and food supply.

The hard-pressed British were not in a position to resist these expanded official contacts between the U.S. and Iran. They feared that the alternative might be further growth of Soviet influence. Besides, the British could hope that American troops and advisers in Iran would absorb some of the local resentment which until then had focused directly upon their own heavy-handed occupation policies. Indeed, by the end of the war the behavior of U.S. troops in Iran, the spotty performance of the U.S. advisory missions, and disappointing levels of direct U.S. economic and military assistance, had all become matters of some contention between the U.S. and Iran.

Unofficial contact between the U.S. and Iran remained low during the war. There was no strong commercial attraction between the two countries, in view of the low wartime demand for Iran's carpets, furs, caviar, and pistachio nuts. Where some attraction might have developed, in the area of petroleum concessions, it again met British and Soviet obstructions. U.S. oil companies were invited once more to seek concessions in Iran in 1943, but Prime Minister Churchill intervened to advise Roosevelt that "a wrangle about oil would be a poor prelude for the tremendous joint enterprise to which we have bound ourselves." Roosevelt felt compelled to give his assurance in reply that the U.S. would not "make sheep's eyes" at British oil interests in Iran.[6] Russia also showed concern by reasserting its own demands for extended oil and mineral rights in the northern part of Iran. Rather than yield to these escalating pressures, the Iranian government cancelled all concession negotiations with outside powers until after the war.[7]

After the war U.S. contact with Iran remained quite tentative. At one point in 1943 Roosevelt had expressed his hope to build a generous postwar policy in Iran "which might be used as a pattern for our relations with all less favored nations."[8] But following the belated Soviet withdrawal from Azerbaijan in 1946, the U.S. returned to its earlier habit of paying deference to Britain in the Near East, and much less heed to Iran.[9] Iran was more eager than ever to build closer contact with the U.S., and in September 1946 the Shah made an urgent request for both economic and military assistance. But military aid was extended only in small quantities, and direct economic aid was denied altogether.[10]

Only following the celebrated nationalization of the Anglo-Iranian Oil Company, in 1951, did U.S. attention turn decisively toward Iran. At first the nationalization crisis only gave the U.S. another reason to refuse assistance to Iran. Great Britain remained Iran's chief antagonist, and the U.S. sought at first to play only a mediatory role. But through its direct role in the removal of Prime Minister Mohammed Mossadeq from power, in August 1953, the U.S. did replace Britain as the dominant Western power in Tehran. After 1953, levels of direct contact between the U.S. and Iran increased dramatically.

First to increase was U.S. aid to Iran. An initial $45 million arrived within one month of the 1953 coup, and in fiscal year 1954, U.S. aid totaled $127 million, more than five times the total for the previous eight-year period. Economic and military assistance continued at a high level for the decade to follow, until the mid-1960s, when the political security of the Shah, and Iran's own increasing petroleum revenues, began to permit a tapering off of direct aid. But by the time a full termination of this aid program was announced in 1967, Iran had received nearly $1 billion in U.S. economic assistance since 1953.[11]

Unofficial economic contact between the U.S. and Iran also increased significantly after 1953. A landmark agreement was negotiated in 1954 to cover re-entry of Western oil companies into Iran. This agreement ended the British monopoly and gave to five U.S. companies (Mobil, Gulf, Standard Oil of California, Standard Oil of New Jersey, and Texaco) a combined 40 per cent of the new Iranian consortium.[12]

Along with aid and investment, U.S. trade with Iran also increased after 1953. In fact, by the late 1950s, excessive imports from the U.S. became such a burden to Iran's economic position that the 1943 trade expansion agreement had to be abrogated. But these momentary difficulties were eased by the increase in Iran's oil revenues in the mid-1960s,[13] and at that point Iranian-American trade began to rise quickly once more, growing at annual rates as high as seven per cent. The U.S. has since attained a position as Iran's leading trading partner.

U.S. business contact with Iran has grown most dramatically since 1971, parallel to the increasing price of petroleum and the sudden availability of surplus "petro-dollars" in the hands of the Iranian government. A U.S. trade center was established in Tehran in 1973, and in the following year the two governments formed a Joint Commission designed to further promote U.S. trade and investment. At that time U.S. non-military exports to Iran were already valued unofficially at about $2 billion. The 27,000 U.S. citizens working in Iran as contract employees by 1974 had actually come to form that nation's second largest ethnic minority group, after the Armenians. In 1976, Iran signed a trade protocol with the U.S. projecting total trade of $52 billion between the two countries over a five-year period, an agreement which Secretary of State Kissinger described as "the largest of its kind ever signed between two countries."[14]

Oil, of course, remains the centerpiece of Iran's commerce with the external world, now including the U.S. As late as 1970, total U.S. petroleum imports stood at only 1.3 million barrels a day, compared to domestic production rates of 9.6 million barrels a day. Less than 3 per cent of these still meager oil imports originated in Iran. But by 1974, U.S. domestic production had slipped to 8.8 million barrels per day, imports had climbed to 3.5 million barrels per day, and more than 13 per cent of these imports now came from Iran.[15] In that year Iran became the third largest supplier of foreign oil to the U.S., after Canada and Nigeria.

U.S. direct investment in Iran also grew to new levels of significance. By 1975 it was valued at well over $1 billion,[16] making the U.S. the largest foreign investor in the country. A 1955 Treaty of Amity and Economic Relations and Consular Rights had paved the way for this high level of direct investment, by offering to U.S. firms a guarantee of "prompt, effective, and adequate" compensation in the event of expropriation. Iran's desire for U.S. investment specifically increased after the adoption of its Fourth Development Plan (1968-1973), which called for nearly half of a required $11 billion in new investments to come from private sources.[17]

Finally, U.S. military exports to Iran have grown in equally dramatic fashion during this recent period since 1971. When the Shah visited the U.S. in 1969, his plan for a massive Iranian military buildup in the Persian Gulf was strongly encouraged, as a suitable response to the withdrawal of British forces. In 1971, the Iranian defense budget increased by 28 per cent, to more than $1.2 billion.[18] But after 1971, as the Shah's oil revenues suddenly increased, his annual defense expenditures could grow even more rapidly to reach an estimated $9.5 billion by 1976.[19] As one feature of this dramatic growth in defense spending, Iranian arms purchases from the U.S. increased from less than $400 million in 1971 to more than $2.5 billion by 1975. The very high dollar value of these military sales reflects a decision taken by President Nixon, in May 1972, to supply Iran with even the most sophisticated weapons systems. Training and maintenance programs associated with these very modern weapons require the additional presence of more than 14,000 U.S. Defense Department personnel in Iran.

To summarize, Iran and the U.S. have quite recently become interconnected and even "interdependent" with one another. Increasing levels of official and unofficial contact, particularly since 1971, have been encouraged by both governments. Former Secretary of State Kissinger, for example, hailed the 1975 Trade Agreement as symbolic of the "interdependence to which both of our countries have been committed."

Yet this interdependence must not be overstated. While the U.S. is Iran's largest trading partner, it still supplies less than 20 per cent of Iran's imports, while purchasing a mere 1 per cent of Iran's exports. And even following the increase in U.S. dependence upon Iranian oil, and upon the Iranian petro-dollar trade, in 1974 total trade with Iran accounted for only 1.8 per cent of U.S. exports and composed only 2 per cent of all U.S. imports.[20]

The U.S. and Iran fall short of reciprocal trade "vulnerability." Iran is somewhat vulnerable due to its heavy reliance on U.S. arms supplies. In 1976, U.S. Senate investigators concluded that Iran could not make effective use of its newly purchased U.S. arms without U.S. support on a day-to-day basis. But Iran does maintain an alternative source of supply in Great Britain, and it has threatened in the past to turn, if necessary, even to the Soviet Union. "We have 10 other markets to provide us with what we need," the Shah has said. "There are people just waiting for that moment." Reacting with displeasure to the increased price of one advanced U.S. weapons system, the Spruance class destroyer, Iran credibly threatened not to purchase additional advanced weapons which the Pentagon wished to sell.[21] Finally, in the face of a U.S. ban on sales of sensitive nuclear technology (a ban which the Shah labeled "incompatible with our sovereignty"), Iran can turn to France and to Germany. Such is the freedom which any paying customer can enjoy in a wide open world arms trade.

U.S. dependence on Iranian oil is even less than that of Iran on U.S. arms. The U.S. economy is surely sensitive to high OPEC prices, as inspired in the past by the Shah himself. But Iran's bargaining power within OPEC is limited, along with its still modest (8.3 per cent in 1975) market share of U.S. imports. Only in the event of another Arab oil embargo might the U.S. feel specific sensations of "dependence" on Iranian oil.

More strictly speaking, relations between the U.S. and Iran fail to satisfy any one of those conditions which Keohane and Nye have offered in their definition of "complex interdependence." First, U.S.-Iranian relations continue to turn on traditional military or security concerns, such as those dealing with alliance relations, arms sales, Persian Gulf security, or the nearby Arab-Israeli confrontation. Non-security issues, particularly petroleum, do assume a prominent place on the agenda. But such issues have remained ultimately subordinate in the calculation of both governments to strategic issues of power among global, regional, and sub-regional actors. Iranian petroleum, in the eyes of U.S. foreign policy leaders, is highly regarded for its security value, as it proved critical to the survival of Israel during the 1973 Middle East war. When challenged on U.S. arms sales to Iran during the televised 1976 election debates, President Ford did not hesitate to stress this paramount security interest:

> Iran is an ally of the U.S.....The history of our relationship with Iran goes back to the days of President Truman, when he decided that it was critically necessary for our own security as well as that of Iran that we should help that country. And Iran has been a good ally. In 1973 when there was an oil embargo Iran did not participate. Iran continued to sell oil to the U.S. I believe that it is in our interest, and in the interest of Israel and Iran...for the U.S. to sell arms to those countries. It is for their security as well as ours.

Second, the U.S. and Iran do not yet enjoy the multiple channels of *reciprocal* trans-national contact which are a pre-requisite for "complex interdependence." The U.S. enjoys much greater informal access to Iran than vice versa. It is true, many senior Iranian officials have studied in the U.S., including Ambassador to the U.S. Ardeshir Zahedi, and a number of cabinet ministers. Also, large numbers of Iranian military officers have been trained either in the U.S. or in Iran by U.S. military advisers. This "Americanization" of Iranian military and political elites continues today (there are currently more than 20,000 Iranian students in the U.S.), and allows the U.S. to influence Iranian politics in a manner sometimes favorable to its own interests.[22] Reciprocal channels of contact maintained by U.S.-trained Iranian officials in their dealings with the U.S. Congress or with the Defense Department do not yet allow comparable access to the levers of power and authority within the U.S. The Shah has admitted that Iranian intelligence agents do keep close watch on Iranian student activities within the U.S. But Iran is not yet in a position to penetrate the U.S. economic or political community to the same degree that the U.S. can penetrate political and economic activities in Tehran. For example, when Iran recently sought to purchase a mere 11-15 percent of the shares of Pan American World Airways, Congressional suspicions were aroused, press opposition developed, and the deal was suspended. As the Shah later complained, the Americans had reacted to Iran "as if we were a microbe invading some beautiful, immaculate thing."

Even the informal access which the U.S. currently enjoys in Iran can be overstated. The Iranian government, once easily corrupted by foreign money and wide open to Western intrigue, is today a more disciplined entity. Iranian officials are under the constant scrutiny of a large security force directly loyal to the Shah. Foreign businessmen, agents, and diplomats can no longer bribe their way into immediate positions of influence in Tehran.[23]

As a third observation, the presence or employment of armed forces plays anything but a "negligible" role in the conduct of U.S.-Iranian relations. During the 1951-53 Anglo-Iranian Oil Company nationalization crisis, some constraints against the use of force did seem to be in evidence. According to Secretary of State Acheson, "In simpler times and places, armed intervention known as 'gunboat diplomacy' would have resolved this problem in favor of the stronger power, but the United Nations Charter put obstacles, to say the least, in the way of that."[24] Yet this same Charter did not prevent the great powers, including the U.S., from using the more sophisticated forceful technique of "covert action" to bring down the Mossadeq government in 1953. The continued availability of such techniques implies something less than mutually constrained conditions of "complex interdependence."[25] As for more conventional military options, the cost of undertaking operations against Iran has indeed increased since 1941, when Britain and Russia invaded and occupied that country in a few days against only token opposition. But much of this increased cost is a direct function of increasing Iranian military capabilities, and so it reflects anything but the diminished importance of armed forces.

So the necessary conditions of "complex interdependence" as described by Keohane and Nye, and as observed in the case of U.S. relations with Canada, are not present in the Iranian case, even though that case has recently developed to produce a high level of U.S.-Iranian contact and interaction. This is because U.S. contact and interaction with Iran has grown primarily through a logic of tentative diplomatic calculation and convenience. As a consequence, it remains to some degree conditioned upon such calculation. As with Iran and Germany before World War II, so with Iran and the U.S. today. Iran's interdependence with the U.S. is not yet founded upon the self-sustaining structures of cultural, geographic, or economic proximity which Keohane and Nye found in relations of "complex interdependence" between the U.S. and Canada.

But here a new question must be raised. In the current partnership of mutual convenience which exists between the U.S. and Iran, does the U.S., as the stronger power, enjoy a larger share of rewards? If U.S.-Iranian relations are conducted in a highly traditional manner, according to calculations of national self-interest, one might expect the stronger power, the U.S., to have the better of the bargain. What follows is a discussion of how and why this has not recently been so.

2. U.S.-Iranian Conflicts, 1920-75: Origins and Outcomes

One means to check the changing distribution of diplomatic advantage between the U.S. and Iran is to review over time the origins and the outcomes of diplomatic conflicts which have occurred between the two countries. These diplomatic conflicts are identified by a strict application of standard criteria developed by Keohane and Nye.[26] In keeping with these criteria, a major U.S.-Iranian conflict is defined as any request or demand communicated from one government to the other, directly or through official channels, not easily or quickly satisfied, and reaching the attention of the President of the U.S. By this standard, 22 conflicts occurred between the U.S. and Iran between 1920 and 1975. Exactly half of these 22 conflicts took place before 1945, and half since 1945. Of the 11 postwar conflicts, 7 took place following the intensification of U.S.-Iranian contact in 1953. All 22 of these major conflicts are summarized, and described as to origin and outcome, in Table 1.

Before reviewing the outcome of these conflicts between 1920 and 1975 two observations must be made with regard to the composition and the formation of this conflict agenda.

TABLE 1

U.S.-Iranian Conflicts on Presidential Agenda: 1920-1975

Primary issue area of conflict	Nation placing conflict on agenda	Conflict outcome closer to objectives of	Conflict Summary
Socio-economic	U.S.	Even	1. North Persian Oil Concession, 1920-25. (Encouraged by U.S. State Department and Iranian government, Standard Oil of New Jersey and later Sinclair sought oil concessions in North Persia. But Iranian demands for a loan, and U.S. reluctance to endorse one company over another, plus opposition from both Britain and Russia, led to breakdown in negotiations. No concessions were granted.)
Diplomatic	U.S.	U.S.	2. Imbrie compensations[a], 1924-26. (Following the killing of U.S. Vice Consul Robert W. Imbrie by an "unprovoked" mob in Tehran, U.S. demanded swift justice and full compensation for Imbrie's widow, threatening otherwise to break relations. Iran met all U.S. demands.)
Socio-economic	Iran	Iran	3. First Millspaugh Mission[a], 1922-27. (Dr. A. C. Millspaugh, a U.S. private citizen, was nominated by U.S., at Iran's request, to serve as financial adviser. Iran later requested that U.S. control Millspaugh's actions, but U.S. instead supported Millspaugh, who finally resigned after Iran reduced his authority.)
Diplomatic	Iran	Iran	4. Elkton Affair[a], 1935-39. (Persian Minister Djalal was arrested for speeding in Elkton, Maryland. Iran protested U.S. media coverage of incident and closed legation in Washington, suspended second-class U.S. mail entering Iran, and threatened to break all economic relations. U.S. cautioned press on delicacy of matter, and after two years finally sent special

[a]Non-state actors, such as transnational organizations, significantly involved.

Primary issue area of conflict	Nation placing conflict on agenda	Conflict outcome closer to objec- tives of	Conflict Summary
			mission to Tehran to satisfy Shah's conditions for return to normal relations.)
Politico- military	Iran	U.S.	5. Military Aircraft Purchase, 1940-41. (Iran learned that military aircraft which it sought to purchase from U.S. increased in price and had been committed to other purchasers ahead of Iran. Iran requested priority over others, and credits from U.S., but without success.)
Politico- military	Iran	U.S.	6. Military Occupation of Iran, 1941-42. (As Britain and Russia threatened occupation of Iran, amid concern over presence of German agents in Tehran, Iran requested good offices of U.S. U.S. viewed struggle against Hitler as more important and only went so far as to request that Britain and Russia be more out-spoken about their "good intentions" in Iran, while the military occupation of Iran was com-pleted.)
Socio- economic	Iran	U.S.	7. Wartime Food Shipments, 1942-43. (Due to disruption of Iranian economy during wartime occupation, Tehran suffered from food shortage. Iran requested food aid from U.S., as it was unable to obtain any from Britain, which had placed heavy conditions on such aid. U.S. deferred to Britain, which de-layed food shipments until Iran made political concessions on other matters.)
Diplomatic	Iran	Iran	8. Sovereignty Guarantee, 1941-43. (Under war-time occupation, Iran requested U.S. signature on treaty with occupying powers, to increase value of "sovereignty" guarantees contained in treaty. U.S., without saying no, delayed. But finally, in 1943 U.S. sponsored 'Tehran Declaration," which placed U.S. "at one" with Iranian desire for postwar independence from foreign powers.)

Primary issue area of conflict	Nation placing conflict on agenda	Conflict outcome closer to objectives of	Conflict Summary
Socio-economic	Iran	U.S.	9. Second Millspaugh Mission[a], 1942-45. (At Iran's request, U.S. nominated private financial adviser to serve in Tehran, again Dr. A. C. Millspaugh. With U.S. backing, Millspaugh then proceeded to assume considerable control over finances of Iran, which prompted ineffective Iranian resistance. Only after a belated curtailment of Millspaugh's authority did he resign.)
Politico-military	Iran	U.S.	10. U.S. Troops in Iran, 1942-45. (When U.S. Army troops entered Iran to operate railway, Iran requested formal agreement to govern their status. U.S. suspected Iran of angling for sovereignty guarantee, or of building a case for postwar aid, and so offered only informal guarantees. At end of war, with departure of U.S. troops imminent, Iran stated that agreement was no longer necessary.)
Socio-economic	U.S.	Even	11. Wartime Oil Concession[a], 1943-44. (To build its ties to U.S., Iran invited U.S. companies to seek new oil concessions. U.S. seeking improved access to Middle East oil, encouraged Sinclair and Standard of N.J. to enter negotiations. But Britain, which controlled all Iranian oil production, expressed concern directly to U.S. Then both Britain and Russia made their own demands for new concessions. To protect itself against escalating demands, Iran cancelled all negotiations until after the war.)
Politico-military	Iran	Iran	12. Allied Troop Withdrawals, 1945-46. (Iran asked U.S. support for a troop withdrawal timetable intended to guarantee the departure of British and Russian troops from Iran. U.S. did not press Britain or Russia to Iran's satisfaction, so Iran took issue to U.N., where

[a]Non-state actors, such as transnational organizations, significantly involved.

Primary issue area of conflict	Nation placing conflict on agenda	Conflict outcome closer to objectives of	Conflict Summary
			U.S., eager to demonstrate the value of the U.N., and now more eager to see Russian troops withdrawn, supported Iran.)
Socio-economic	Iran	U.S.	13. Postwar Development Assistance[b], 1947-53. (Iran requested U.S. support for World Bank credits and for direct aid to support new Iranian development plan. U.S. replied that it could only support a "well conceived" plan, and withheld support. When Iran later nationalized Anglo-Iranian Oil Company, U.S. reaffirmed that Iran was not a worthy aid recipient. U.S. finally extended aid to Iran in quantity after overthrow of Mossadeq government.)
Socio-economic	U.S.	U.S.	14. Anglo-Iranian Oil Co. Nationalization[ab], 1950-53. (When Iran nationalized the Anglo-Iranian Oil Company, U.S. entered picture as formal mediator, but also lent informal support to oil company strategy of boycott of nationalized Iranian oil. Boycott placed U.S. in league with Britain, as opposed to Mossadeq nationalization policy, and contributed to final downfall of Mossadeq government.)
Politico-military	U.S.	U.S.	15. Mossadeq Replacement[b], 1951-53. (Britain first suggested to U.S. finding an alternative to the Mossadeq government in Iran. U.S. resisted, so long as Mossadeq appeared to be a genuine nationalist and the best alternative to Communism. But when, after February 1953, Mossadeq launched attack on Shah and Army, U.S. feared growing influence of Communists in Tehran and moved by covert action to speed replacement of Mossadeq government.)
Socio-economic	U.S.	Even	16. Oil Consortium Agreement[a], 1952-54. (U.S. first proposed that American companies purchase and market Iranian oil, as means to com-

[a]Non-state actors, such as transnational organizations, significantly involved.
[b]Conflict of substantial or major proportions.

Primary issue area of conflict	Nation placing conflict on agenda	Conflict outcome closer to objectives of	Conflict Summary
			promise with Mossadeq government over AIOC nationalization. Iran did not approve of idea until fall of Mossadeq, and even then resisted full return to prenationalization conditions.)
Diplomatic	Iran	Iran	17. Cold War Alliance, 1955-59. (After joining Baghdad Pact in 1955, without U.S. encouragement, Iran went on to seek U.S. adherence to that pact as indirect means to obtain formal Cold War alliance with U.S. and greater assistance. Following 1958 revolution in Iraq, and after an Iranian threat to form closer ties with Russia, the U.S. did in 1959 extend a direct security guarantee to Iran.)
Diplomatic	U.S.	Iran	18. Amini Internal Reforms, 1959-62. (U.S. urged Shah to widen his base of political support. Shah moved to create a "two-party system" and appointed a close friend of U.S., Amini, as Premier. Again following U.S. advice, Iran then initiated economic austerity program. But, unable to obtain greater economic aid from the U.S., Shah forced Amini to resign and resisted further internal interference from U.S.)
Politico-military	U.S.	U.S.	19. Extraterritorial Privileges, 1962-64. (Under Defense Department urgings, U.S. formally requested that military personnel in Iran be granted full diplomatic immunity. Iran did not immediately comply. But after obtaining credit for U.S. arms purchases, Iran did approve extension of extraterritorial privileges to U.S. military.)
Politico-military	Iran	Iran	20. F-4D Aircraft Sales, 1965-67. (Iran requested purchase of F-4D military aircraft. U.S. did

Primary issue area of conflict	Nation placing conflict on agenda	Conflict outcome closer to objectives of	Conflict Summary
			not wish Iran to divert funds from development, and also feared antagonizing Egypt, and at first refused sale. But when Shah entered into arms barter deal with Russia, U.S., fearing that Iran might continue to go elsewhere for military equipment, finally offered to sell F-4Ds to Iran.)
Socio-economic	U.S.	Iran	21. Tehran Oil Price Negotiations[a], 1970-71. (Upon hearing OPEC threats to cut off oil supply if major oil companies failed to meet demands, U.S. sent special mission to Tehran to express U.S. concern. But Iran convinced U.S. that threat was not aimed at U.S., only at the private companies, whereupon U.S. backed away from supporting them in Tehran oil price negotiations.)
Socio-economic	U.S.	Iran	22. OPEC Pricing Policy[a], 1973-75. (In 1973, OPEC, led by Iran, agreed upon dramatic increase in price of petroleum. By 1974, U.S. was demanding reduction in price. U.S. and Iran traded public threats over severity of crisis. At OPEC meeting in 1975, OPEC prices were increased once more, at Iran's insistence, in defiance of U.S. requests.)

[a]Non-state actors, such as transnational organizations, significantly involved.

Composition of Conflict Agenda

First, note from Table 2 that the *functional* distribution of issues on this conflict agenda has actually changed very little since 1920. Socio-economic conflicts have held a prominent position overall. They have also held a prominent position during each one of the four historical sub-periods which will be used here to clarify the evolution of U.S.-Iranian relations. Traditional politico-military concerns and great power rivalries did play a dominant role in structuring the *context* of Iran's conflict relations with the U.S. But the day-to-day *substance* of those conflict relations has been formed, most often, from a variety of economic concerns. For example, issues related to oil and to economic assistance were prominent before, during, and after World War II. Such economic issues may have only recently emerged as matters of "high politics" in U.S. relations with some other nations,[27] but they have always held a prominent position on the conflict agenda between the U.S. and Iran.

TABLE 2

Functional Distribution of U.S.-Iranian Conflicts on Presidential Agenda 1920-1975

	Politico-military[a]	Diplomatic[b]	Socio-economic	Total
1920-41[c]	1	2	2	5
1942-45	2	1	3	6
1946-53	2	0	2	4
1954-75	2	2	3	7
1920-1975	7	5	10	22

[a]Force or weaponry involved.

[b]Military force not involved.

[c]Conflict dated by final year of appearance
on presidential agenda.

Agenda Formation

Regarding the formation of this conflict agenda, how did such socio-economic issues consistently attract the attention of the foreign policy leadership? One might at first assume that the frequency of socio-economic conflict was a result of non-state actors engaged in "transnational" initiatives. For example, large private oil companies based in the U.S. but operating in Iran may have been strong enough to push economic conflict issues of their own making onto the diplomatic agenda.

But here a second cautioning observation must be made. Non-state or "transnational" actors have actually played only a modest role in creating conflicts between the U.S. and Iran. Non-state actors, such as the major international oil companies, were significantly involved in eight of the ten socio-economic conflicts on the agenda since 1920. But they contributed to the initiation of only two of these eight conflicts: the Anglo-Iranian Oil Company nationalization dispute and the Tehran oil price negotiations conflict. And of all twenty-two conflicts noted since 1920, including non-economic conflicts, non-state actors contributed to the initiation of only four.

This very modest transnational contribution to agenda formation squares with the earlier observation that U.S.-Iranian relations are not characterized by conditions of "complex interdependence." In the case of U.S.-Canadian relations, as observed by Keohane and Nye, conditions of fully developed "complex interdependence" did permit transnational actors to play a more prominent role in conflict agenda formation.

This is not to dismiss entirely the role of non-state actors in U.S.-Iranian relations as "conflict catalysts." To further clarify this role, consider those two "atypical" cases in which private international oil companies did act as such catalysts: the nationalization of the Anglo-Iranian Oil Company (AIOC) of 1950-53, and the Tehran negotiations of 1970-71. The AIOC case is of such great individual importance that it may indicate a pivotal role for transnational actors in creating conflicts even under conditions which fall short of "complex interdependence." Yet the Tehran negotiations case, a more recent case, does tend to reconfirm the overall judgment that non-state actors perform a modest initiating role in the vast majority of U.S.-Iranian conflicts.

AIOC Nationalization

In the AIOC nationalization dispute, non-state actors did contribute to the development of a highly significant U.S.-Iranian conflict. To begin with, the Anglo-Iranian company invited its own nationalization by refusing to consider Iranian requests for a rate of royalty payment commensurate with that received by other oil-producing states in the Middle East at the time. It is significant that AIOC took this uncompromising stand against the wishes of all major governments involved, including the British government.[28] Following the Iranian nationalization of AIOC in May 1951, the British government did move to fully support the company's interests, by breaking commercial and diplomatic relations with Iran and by threatening at one point to restore British ownership by force of arms. The U.S. cautioned Britain against such a move, as Washington sought for the first year of this crisis to avoid any conflict of its own with the Iranian government.

But a severe conflict between the U.S. and Iran was already developing, outside of formal diplomatic channels. Soon after the nationalization, the major international oil companies, led by AIOC, organized a worldwide boycott against the purchase of nationalized Iranian oil. Despite its mediatory role in the crisis, the U.S. government indirectly took moves to support this company boycott, through participation in the Foreign Petroleum Emergency Committee, a semi-official 19-company association chaired by the Vice President of Standard Oil of New Jersey.[29] The announced purpose of the committee was to protect the Korean War mobilization plan against the possible "loss" of Iranian oil. Of course, Iran was so eager to sell its nationalized oil that such a loss was from the start largely hypothetical. The main task of the committee was a coordinated expansion of oil production outside Iran to facilitate enforcement of the boycott. As L. P. Ellwell-Sutton explains, the Foreign Petroleum Emergency Committee "was in fact an ingenious device to gain official blessing for the general policy of the international oil cartel."[30]

This private company plan, as it came to be supported by Great Britain and eventually by the U.S., prevented Iran from producing, refining, or selling any of its nationalized oil for a period of two years.[31] Prime Minister Mossadeq did not immediately collapse in the face of this boycott, but he did become more hostile to the West, including now the U.S., and more desperate in his efforts to maintain power. In 1953, his growing dependence upon the communist Tudeh party in Tehran, and his efforts to exclude the monarch and the army from Iranian politics, brought on a political as well as an economic crisis, one which appeared from Washington to threaten the Cold War interests of the U.S. Mossadeq was removed in August, with covert assistance from the C.I.A. His successors immediately announced a more compliant policy toward Western oil company interests.

The AIOC nationalization conflict does constitute one highly visible example of a transnational organization (the private international oil cartel) maneuvering sovereign governments (the U.S. and Iran) into a situation of unwanted high-level conflict. But in view of subsequent events relating specifically to Iranian oil, this case remains an exceptional instance of transnational control in the creation of interstate conflict.

The Tehran Negotiations

Private oil companies again played a significant role in the creation of the 1971 Tehran negotiations conflict. But in this case the conflict proved to be of modest proportions, of brief duration, and ultimately disadvantageous to the interests of the companies.

This second case actually had its origins in a *non*-conflict between the two governments over company production rates. In 1966 the Shah began to pressure the companies to increase rates of production in Iran, as one means to increase revenues for his own Government. The companies at first resisted, fearing an oil "glut" and an adverse effect on world prices. But in March 1968, after the 1967 Middle East war oil scare and following the British decision to withdraw from "East of Suez," the U.S. State Department intervened. Under Secretary Eugene Rostow called oil company representatives to the State Department in Washington and cautioned them "not to antagonize the Shah." The companies eventually increased rates of production in Iran in compliance with the coordinated pressure from both Washington and Tehran.[32]

But Iran's pressure on the company cartel was only beginning to increase, as the Shah now turned his attention to oil prices. In December 1970, Iran sponsored a new OPEC agreement which called for higher posted prices and which threatened a halt on all production if the companies failed to meet this demand.[33] At this point the private companies were able momentarily to win a more sympathetic hearing from the U.S. State Department. Mr. John J. McCloy, acting as legal representative of the companies, met with Secretary William P. Rogers on January 15, 1971, and emphasized the danger of this new OPEC challenge. At McCloy's suggestion, Rogers decided to dispatch Under Secretary John Irwin to the Middle East to express "official concerns" directly to the Shah, and to serve formal notice that any nation cutting off oil deliveries to the U.S. or to her allies "would find its relations with the U.S. severely and adversely affected."[37] Once more the oil companies, as non-state actors, had provoked a diplomatic dispute between the U.S. and Iran.

But, in keeping with the larger conclusion drawn from this study, these "transnational" oil company tactics eventually met considerable frustration at the hands of the two governments. When Under Secretary Irwin reached Tehran he promptly accepted a disarming assurance from the Shah that the OPEC threat to cut off oil had been directed solely against the private companies, and not against the consuming nations themselves. Irwin then went so far as to endorse the Shah's own preference for separating price agreements in the Persian Gulf from the possibility of future price increases in the Mediterranean. This U.S. failure to endorse price stability contributed directly to the outcome of the 1971 Tehran negotiations: a price increase considered by the companies to be almost ruinous, exposing as it did the weakness of their private cartel. Having inspired the Irwin mission, and having pushed their preferred issue to the top of the diplomatic conflict agenda, the private companies finally found themselves isolated and disadvantaged in a conflict resolution process controlled by the two governments.

Direction of Conflict Outcomes

The most dramatic change to be noted in the recent history of U.S.-Iranian conflict lies neither in the composition of the conflict agenda nor in the role which transnational organizations have played in its formation. Instead, that change is found in the *direction* of conflict outcome. During the most recent period under study, 1954-75, Iran prevailed in 5 of its 7 conflicts with the U.S. Before 1954, conflict outcomes came closer to Iranian objectives in only 4 cases out of 15.

At first it seems curious that Iran should do better in conflict relations with the U.S. only *following* the covert intervention of 1953, just as the U.S. had finally become the dominant foreign power in Tehran. A similar weak state advantage in post-war conflict outcome was identified by Keohane and Nye in their pilot study of U.S. relations with Canada.[35] But Iran's advantage is not immediately clarified by this Canadian example. Recall that Iran, unlike Canada, did not enjoy conditions of "complex interdependence" with the U.S., even in recent years. Instead, Iran managed to secure its relative advantage in conflict outcome within the confines of a traditional alliance relationship.

Iran's record of success in recent conflict relations with the U.S. is in part a function of its alliance relationship with the U.S. Robert Keohane, writing in an earlier context, has observed that small allies, such as Iran, can gain considerable leverage by threatening to "move toward neutra-

TABLE 3

Directions of Outcome in U.S.-Iranian Conflicts on Presidential Agenda, 1920-1975

OUTCOME FAVORED

	U.S.	Iran	Even	Total
1920-41	2	2	1	5
1942-45	4	1	1	6
1946-53	3	1	0	4
1954-75	1	5	1	7
1920-75	10	9	3	22

lism."[36] Such threats have indeed been one of Iran's most effective alliance tactics since 1954, but by no means its only effective tactic.

Before Iran became a Cold War client state, that is, before 1953, its options were limited in conflict relations with the U.S. Iran could not pressure the U.S. with threats of "movement toward neutralism," because Iran was, in effect, already neutral. What is more, Iran was at that time a disaffected client of Great Britain. The U.S. felt little responsibility and showed little patience for Iran's grievances. For these reasons it was Mossadeq's greatest error, at the climax of the AIOC nationalization crisis, to warn President Eisenhower in a personal letter that Iran might turn to the Soviet Union for aid if U.S. assistance was not forthcoming.[37] Eisenhower rejected this appeal, and within three months Mossadeq had been removed from power in Tehran, in part through the actions of the C.I.A.

While suffering this dramatic loss of autonomy, Iran did gain in one respect after 1953. Iran was suddenly in a better position to engage the protective instincts of its new distant and wealthy patron, the U.S. Iran could now employ threats of "moving toward neutralism" to great advantage.

The Shah tested this new advantage immediately, in February 1954, when he let it be known that Soviet petroleum experts were welcome in Tehran to compete with Western oil companies for whatever concession the new government might offer to foreign operators. The Western companies, which had been demanding only the most favorable terms for entering a new Iranian consortium, were at first unmoved. But with the hint of Soviet competition, the U.S. State Department applied new pressure on the U.S. companies to conclude their negotiations, and an agreement generally satisfactory to Iran was reached in August.[38] The same tactic which had brought down Mossadeq one year earlier was now working to the advantage of the Shah.

Iran enhanced its new tactical advantage by joining the Baghdad Pact in October 1955. The U.S. had not encouraged this move, fearing that Iran's formal membership in a Western alliance would only increase U.S. financial responsibility for the weak and impoverished Iranian government, while unnecessarily antagonizing the Soviet Union. These anxieties were not totally unfounded; Iran reinforced its claim on U.S. aid and U.S. security protection by strengthening its formal ties with the Northern Tier group. And to exercise those claims, once again, it periodically threatened to move back "toward neutralism" and in the direction of the Soviet Union. Early in 1959 the Shah served notice that the Soviets had offered him "unlimited aid" on condition that he *not* conclude a bilateral security agreement directly with the U.S. He had long been seeking such a direct agreement, without success. The Shah's threat was made credible when a Soviet negotiating team actually arrived in Tehran. At this point the U.S. hastened to make new concessions on the terms of its assistance relations with Iran, and signed a bilateral security pact in March of the same year.[39]

As late as 1966 Iran was still using this threat of "ties to Russia" as an effective means of increasing its leverage in Washington. At that time the Shah was seeking to purchase modern F-4D fighter aircraft from the U.S. It was U.S. policy to discourage such arms sales as the possible prelude to a new arms race in the Persian Gulf, and as incompatible with Iranian development needs. But early in 1966 the Shah hinted of his plans to "go elsewhere" if the U.S. remained unwilling to meet his major military requirements. To underline this threat he actually concluded an initial $10 million "arms barter" deal with the Soviet Union. At that, President Johnson decided to supply F-4Ds to Iran.[40]

As U.S.-Soviet tensions subsequently began to relax, these threats of "moving toward Russia" became a less effective instrument of leverage. But Iran then found that its security alliance with the U.S. could be manipulated in other ways. First, when the British decided in 1968 to withdraw military forces from the Persian Gulf, Iran was able to solicit arms from the U.S. on a promise to become a friendly substitute for British power, the new "force for stability" in the region. And beyond the Gulf as well, by offering tacit support for U.S. policies in Indochina and by maintaining cooperative commercial relations with Israel, Iran found additional means to profit by playing a new role, that of "dutiful ally."

It cost the Shah little to fulfill these alliance duties, but it has paid handsome rewards. As noted earlier, the State Department specifically advised U.S. oil companies to increase Iranian production in 1968 so as "not to antagonize the Shah." And recall that a similar State Department attitude worked to Iran's advantage at the time of the 1971 Tehran negotiations, when the Irwin mission quickly yielded to the Shah's assurance on oil stoppages, willingly endorsing his price negotiation strategy. Washington has been prepared to satisfy the Shah on oil to maintain his "dutiful" posture of strength in the Persian Gulf and diplomatic support elsewhere.

The 1973-75 conflict over OPEC pricing policy offers the best illustration of this new Iranian advantage. During the 1973 Middle East War, and throughout the subsequent Arab oil embargo, the Shah continued to supply petroleum to the U.S. and to Israel, on the grounds that he was "not mixing business with politics."[41] The U.S. sought to reward this forbearance, even though it cost the Shah nothing at all. Refusing to mix business with politics was in this instance merely good business. More recently, the Shah was officially credited with using his "ability to talk with both Israel and the Arab countries" to help Secretary of State Kissinger to pursue his successful efforts at "shuttle diplomacy."[42] In return, Washington was once again more tolerant of Iran's promotion of higher oil prices within OPEC.

Iran first cultivated this image of the dutiful ally by its steadfast refusal to criticize U.S. policy in Indochina. Throughout the long diplomatic nightmare of Vietnam, U.S. policymakers could look forward to their dealings with the Shah, who withheld all adverse comment and who even flattered American statesmen with praise for their Third World security policies.[43] Even to the very end, the Shah found occasion to profit from this tactic. While visiting the U.S. in May 1975, he went out of his way to publicly congratulate President Ford for "great leadership" and for "not shrinking in front of events" in the Mayaguez affair.[44] It was coincidentally noted by one account that President Ford "never so much as mentioned the oil price issue" in his various discussions with the Shah during this same 1975 state visit.[45]

So, by supporting the U.S. on matters of great importance to Washington such as Israel or Indochina, Iran was able to gain nearly a free hand on other issues, such as oil prices, arms sales, or even C.I.A. support—and then abandonment—of the Kurdish rebellion in Iraq. This new "loyal ally" advantage, added to the earlier advantage derived from "threats to move toward neutralism," accounts for much of Iran's success in controlling the direction of conflict outcome in dealings with the U.S. after 1953.

But this Iranian success requires qualification in two important respects. First, Iran enjoyed most if its advantage in *low-intensity* conflicts within *non-politico-military* issue areas. And second, Iran's *relative* success seldom forced more than a *relative* disadvantage onto the U.S. In most recent conflicts, Iran may have gained more, but the U.S., by any *absolute* standard, gained at the same time.

Concerning the first of these qualifications, observe in Table 1 that Iran has tended to win *low-intensity* conflicts within *diplomatic* or *socio-economic* issue areas, while the U.S. has consistently won all *high-intensity* conflicts and a majority of all *politico-military* conflicts. This is some vindication for the traditional view that high-priority, high-intensity issues will tend to be resolved to the advantage of the stronger power. While Iran has done well in conflicts with the U.S. since 1954, this is in part because low-priority, low-intensity conflicts dominated the diplomatic agenda during much of that period.

The second, and more important, point is that most U.S.-Iranian conflict outcomes since 1954, while favoring Iran in a relative sense, have actually been characterized by a pattern of *joint gains.* One nation may profit more than the other, but, typically, neither nation has experienced an unacceptable setback. Such joint gains help to sustain an alliance relationship which otherwise offers a disproportionate advantage to Iran, the junior partner.

3. The Evolution and Preservation of Joint Gains in U.S.-Iranian Conflict

Before 1953, conflicts between the U.S. and Iran were more intense, and were seldom resolved to the simultaneous advantage of both governments. Particularly during the Mossadeq period, the U.S. and Iran engaged in a sequence of *joint loss* conflicts. The protracted postwar dispute over U.S. assistance to Iran proved disadvantageous to both parties. The U.S. "won" this dispute, but by limiting aid to Iran it actually sacrificed a low-cost opportunity to maintain a working relationship with the nationalist government in Tehran. The only gain may have been some momentary favor with Great Britain. The AIOC nationalization dispute likewise produced benefits for neither party. The State Department, following the lead of the British Foreign Office and the private oil cartel, mismanaged this crisis to the disadvantage of both Washington and Tehran.[46] The U.S. eventually "won" its conflict with Mossadeq, to be sure, but in doing so it felt little sense of positive achievement. Secretary of State Acheson recalls this period of conflict with Iran as "a tragic affair," and faults his own department for having "fumbled the ball."[47]

But after 1953, with Great Britain removed from its dominant position in Tehran, and with Iran now a Cold War client of the U.S., the two governments were finally able to conduct their relations to much greater mutual advantage. For example, the 1954 oil consortium conflict produced something of a joint victory. The U.S. secured a valuable 40 per cent share in the new consortium, while Iran finally broke Britain's monopoly control in oil without having to sacrifice the formal claim to national ownership established by Mossadeq. Continuing this pattern of joint gains, the 1959 security pact served the Cold War interests of the U.S. even while it offered greater advantages in the form of security and assistance to Iran. Likewise, the Amini reforms conflict in the early 1960s produced some gains for the U.S., in the form of modest Iranian military cutbacks and improved economic planning, while the Shah won his own victory in the more critical area of limiting Iranian "democratization" and on the larger principle of foreign non-interference. Similarly, the 1965-67 conflict over F-4D aircraft sales produced an agreement eventually seen as profitable by both parties. The sales meant a larger export market, more efficient production runs for U.S. defense industries, and an improved U.S. trade balance, even while they enhanced the Shah's security position in the Persian Gulf. The sense of mutual advantage to be gained from Iran's purchase of sophisticated U.S. arms eventually came to be accepted as an article of faith by both governments. As one final instance of joint gains in recent U.S.-Iranian conflict, even the 1971 Tehran agreement, while clearly advantageous to Iran in the matter of an oil price increase, was nonetheless satisfying to many in the U.S. government who had sought, above all, to avoid an OPEC oil "cutoff."[48]

On the strength of such joint gains, the U.S.-Iranian alliance has endured, despite the larger relative advantage which this alliance seems to offer to the weaker party, Iran. Perceptions of common benefit grew, particularly during the Nixon-Kissinger period. In 1975, despite continuing differences over oil prices, Secretary of State Kissinger observed that relations between the two countries "had probably never been better."[49] Assistant Secretary Alfred L. Atherton vowed that the relationship which governed relations between the U.S. and Iran was "a very special one" and would "develop and expand into new areas" to bring "ever increasing benefits to the American and the Iranian people."[50]

4. Threats to the Special Relationship: Temptations of Issue Linkage

The special relationship between the U.S. and Iran is not so durable as these official statements suggest. First of all, that relationship has rested heavily, since 1953, upon personal direction of Iranian foreign policy by the Shah himself. There are those in his silenced opposition who either disapprove of close alliance with the U.S., or who would be less adept at managing that alliance. The foreign policy which the Shah now directs will be tested by his eventual passing from the scene.

But even with the Shah in power, Iran's special relationship with the U.S. has recently encountered a new strain. This strain is in part the natural by-product of increased contact, and of expanding the special relationship into "new areas." But this strain also derives from a recent *decline* in joint gains to be realized from U.S.-Iranian conflict outcomes.

The 1973-75 OPEC pricing conflict, the most recent of those considered in this study, is a case in point. By any standard the U.S. "lost" this conflict. Its own economic recovery, and worldwide recovery, lagged against the continued high price for OPEC oil. Secretary Kissinger had argued that the stability of the international system itself required a price reduction. "The world cannot sustain even the present level of prices, much less continuing increases," he observed. "What has gone up by political decision can be reduced by political decision."[51] Iran's direct rejection of this clearly stated U.S. position mixed diplomatic insult with commercial injury.

Iran "won" this conflict by engineering a 10 per cent OPEC price increase in October 1975, despite U.S. assertions that oil prices ought to — come down. Yet beneath the appearance of victory, Iran's own circumstances were scarcely improved by this new price increase. Western demand for Iranian oil was already severely depressed after two years of very high prices, and revenues from oil exports were falling well short of programmed expenditures. Iran had spent its way into a requirement for higher revenues which still higher prices, in the long run, might not deliver. But in the short run, higher prices were the only means available. A pattern of joint losses, amid increasing levels of conflict, had replaced the earlier pattern of joint gains.[52]

Such a pattern of joint loss can introduce instability into a pattern of bilateral relations. As Keohane and Nye explain, "...international regimes can be changed if they become intolerable to states that have overwhelming underlying power."[53] By 1975 the U.S. might have seen fit to initiate such a change, to avoid continuing loss in the dispute with Iran over oil prices. For example, the U.S. might have violated the spirit of its special relationship with Iran, by resorting to tactics of "issue linkage." To back up its demand for lower oil prices, the U.S. might have threatened to curtail its commercial exports to the still developing Iranian economy, to reconsider its arms transfer policies, or even to withdraw its security guarantees. In the face of declining benefits from its alliance relationship with Iran, the U.S. might have simply threatened to stop paying the "leadership costs" which helped to maintain that relationship.[54]

Such expectations notwithstanding, the U.S. resisted these linkage temptations. For example, when Secretary Kissinger was asked in November 1974 whether U.S. food sales to Iran would be "linked" to oil, he replied, "No, the issue of food supply has not been linked with the issue of energy supply...At least as far as Iran and the U.S. are concerned, this is not a problem."[55] Even at the height of the 1975 oil pricing dispute, the U.S. pledged not to employ linkage tactics in conflict relations with Iran. In December 1975, Assistant Secretary of State Atherton observed that "we have differed with Iran on the issue of oil prices; but both our governments have determined that this difference should not stand in the way of cooperation in other areas to our mutual benefit..."[56]

Some officials within the U.S. foreign policy leadership did advocate a linkage strategy, even though Iran had never joined the Arab oil boycott. Secretary of Defense James R. Schlesinger allegedly sought retaliation following the Shah's 1973 oil price increase by sharply increasing Iran's share of the research and development costs involved in F-14 production.[57] And late in 1976, on the eve of yet another OPEC price increase, Treasury Secretary William Simon advocated licensing and even termination of some U.S. food and arms sales to Iran, through invocation of the "Trading with the Enemy Act." But Secretary of State Kissinger (although once identified as an advocate of linkage) repeatedly vetoed this response to the oil price dispute with Iran.[58]

In the post-Kissinger era, with congressional and presidential opposition to international arms sales on the rise, with the oil pricing dispute as yet unresolved, and in view of its more outspoken policy on human rights violations, the new foreign policy leadership in Washington might have been expected to show less forbearance in its relations with Iran.

But through its first few months in power, the Carter Administration did not substantially alter the terms of U.S.-Iranian relations. In May 1977, following his first meeting with the Shah, Secretary of State Cyrus Vance was asked if the U.S. would now "link" arms sales to human rights. "No such linkage has been discussed," Vance replied. Only two weeks earlier, the new administration had authorized an $850 million sale of advanced military surveillance aircraft (AWACS) to Iran despite congressional opposition. At a CENTO meeting in Tehran, also in May, American officials indicated privately that they considered the trend in Iranian civil liberties policy to be "favorable," and that any economic or diplomatic sanctions against the Shah were virtually out of the question.[59] President Carter welcomed the Shah to Washington in November 1977 with a reaffirmation of the special diplomatic relationship between the two countries and with a pledge "to work closely with Congress in meeting Iran's security needs."

Iran has bravely served notice that it would not fear a U.S. attempt to employ linkage. In March 1976 the Shah observed that he could hurt the U.S. "as badly if not more so than you can hurt us. Not just through oil: we can create trouble for you in the region. If you force us to change our friendly attitude, the repercussions will be immeasurable."[60] Little credibility may be given to such threats, but a larger explanation is still due for the U.S. reluctance, until now, to employ linkage tactics in its relations with Iran. Perhaps the Shah's promise to "show sympathy" and to give the U.S. "a break" late in 1977 by resisting another oil price increase contributed to President Carter's forbearance. But it is also noteworthy that this forbearance persists despite an absence of "complex interdependence" in U.S.-Iranian relations.

Keohane and Nye observed a similar inhibition against issue linkage in the case of U.S. relations with Canada, and attributed it, in part, to the presence of "complex interdependence."[61] Consider briefly the possibility that such an inhibition exists in the Iranian case in part because U.S. interdependence with Iran is *not* yet "complex."

In the U.S.-Canadian case, specific organized domestic interest groups within the U.S. did find themselves threatened, at times, either by Canadian commercial competition or by Canadian economic nationalism. Keohane and Nye have argued that these groups were *not* generally successful in generating "from below" an official U.S. policy of retaliatory "linkage" toward Canada.[62] But U.S. interaction with Canada did at least present a mix of threat as well as opportunity to some organized U.S. domestic interests. In the Iranian case, organized interest groups within the U.S. did *not* feel individually threatened by Iranian human rights policies or by the high price of OPEC oil, a price paid by all. They at least found it difficult to relate that high price to the behavior of any one foreign nation such as Iran. So Iranian oil policy did not inspire organized interest articulation "from below" within the U.S. political system.

In fact, Iran makes itself most visible to powerful and well-placed political actors within the U.S. not by selling its high-priced oil but by spending welcome quantities of money. U.S. arms manufacturers, farmers, exporting firms, lawyers, consultants, even universities—all have done lucrative business with Iran. Among groups such as these, Canada was highly visible to buyers as well as to sellers, to consumers as well as producers, and to employers as well as employees. By contrast, U.S. economic ties with Iran are not so variable or so complex, and in their simplicity they seldom pose a well-focused threat to organized domestic interest groups within the U.S. So an impetus "from below" to initiate retaliatory linkage tactics against Iran has not developed.

This study concludes that the governments of both Iran and the U.S. came to profit from their relations with each other, particularly after the U.S. assumed a dominent role in organizing the conduct of those relations in 1953. By entering into a Cold War alliance with Iran, the U.S. realized important benefits, primarily in the conduct of its anti-Soviet security policies, but later also in the regional politics of the Persian Gulf, in Arab-Israeli affairs, and perhaps even in support for its policies in Vietnam. The client government in Iran also gained from this alliance relationship. The Shah received important security guarantees, internal as well as external, his government was given substantial military and economic aid for a decade, and somewhat later he gained a "freer hand" in the conduct of policies critical to Iran's own security and economic development. This Iranian advantage extended even to the conduct of conflict relations. First, by threatening to weaken the alliance, and later by posing as a "loyal ally," Iran was able to prevail in the majority of its recent conflicts with the U.S., including the continuing dispute over the high price of OPEC oil. This Iranian advantage has not yet inspired effective U.S. action to alter the current regime. As late as 1978 perceptions of mutual advantage were still dominant among foreign policy elites within the two governments.

It should be emphasized that this perception of mutual advantage did *not* consistently extend beyond the foreign policy-making elites. Some U.S. citizens who pay higher energy costs may not agree with their government that a healthy military and political alliance with Iran is adequate compensation for their own financial discomfort. And many within Iran have a strong case for questioning the final value of their government's special relationship with the U.S. After all, that relationship was first established through covert U.S. support for a royalist-military coup against the authority of their own parliamentary leaders. And that relationship has continued in frustrating Iran's constitutionalist ambitions. The "joint gains" preserved in the current U.S.-Iranian relationship may therefore diverge from a larger calculation of joint *popular* interest. But for the political leaders of the two governments, the joint gains realized since 1953 are no less real and no less an argument for maintaining the present relationship.

In its comparative aspect, this study supports one additional conclusion. U.S. relations with Iran were not grounded in conditions of "complex interdependence" such as those observed by Keohane and Nye in their discussion of U.S.-Canadian relations. And yet, since 1953, U.S.-Iranian relations did exhibit many of the characteristics associated with complex interdependence, including a conflict agenda dominated by non-military issues, inhibitions against cross-issue linkage, and patterns of conflict outcome generally favoring Iran, the "weaker" power.

It seems that there is more than one way for the weak to profit from the rules of the game. U.S. relations with Iran have not become "Canadianized." The traditional rules of power calculation among sovereign states remain in force. Economic issues tend to dominate the conflict agenda *not* because military security matters have become less important to the relationship, but because most security matters were resolved beyond challenge by the rules themselves, which the U.S. imposed by force in 1953. Conflict outcomes often favor the weaker party *not* because of some new advantage offered to Iran by multiple channels of contact or by a dynamic of "complex interdependence." Instead, U.S. diplomacy offers this advantage to Iran in order to better preserve those patterns of joint gain which are perceived in the relationship. And issue linkage strategies fail to emerge in U.S. policy despite Iran's greater success in conflict outcome, *not* because any force borne of complex interdependence resists that emergence. Instead, linkages fail to form in part because U.S. economic ties with Iran are *not* yet complex, because few well organized interest groups within the U.S. feel individually threatened by Iran. One group which did feel so threatened, the private U.S. oil companies, failed in their brief attempt in 1971 to muster official support from the State Department.

So, some of the *expectations* earlier associated with conditions of complex interdependence are fulfilled in the case of U.S.-Iranian relations, despite an absence of complex interdependence. This leads to a suspicion that the major dynamic at work in U.S.-Iranian relations, a more traditional dynamic of U.S. leadership in maintenance of a world-wide alliance system, can under certain circumstances produce effects which favor smaller or weaker powers no less than conditions of complex interdependence.

NOTES

[1]This early "transnational" contact was later extended to the U.S., when many Assyrian mission students from Iran emigrated to the Chicago area, where more than 60,000 of their descendants still live.

[2]Secretary of State Hughes warned President Coolidge in 1923 that such measures would invite "difficulties with other governments." See *Foreign Relations of the United States*, 1923, Volume II, p. 717.

[3]The U.S. press speculated at the time that the killing of Vice Consul Robert Imbrie, by an "unprovoked street mob," was actually the doing of Soviet agents. Imbrie was a decorated veteran of five separate intelligence missions into the Soviet Union, and was known to be on the Cheka "death list." With the Soviets anxious to prevent an American oil concession in North Persia, it was logical for some news reporters to suspect that Soviet agents had been involved. See *New York Times*, July 22, 1924, p. 5:1.

[4]See Mark H. Lytle, "American-Iranian Relations, 1941-47, and the Redefinition of National Security," unpublished Ph.D. Dissertation, Yale Universtiy, 1973, pp. 11-14.

[5]See *Foreign Relations of the U.S.*, 1941, Volume III, p. 419.

[6]*Foreign Relations of the U.S.*, 1944, Volume III, p. 100.

[7]*Foreign Relations of the U.S.*, 1944, Volume V, p. 455

[8]*Foreign Relations of the U.S.*, 1943, Volume IV, p. 420n.

[9]Dean Acheson, *Present at the Creation* (New York: W.W. Norton & Co., Inc., 1969), p. 646.

[10]In October 1950, after a four-year delay, the U.S. finally extended one-tenth of the economic aid which Iran originally requested, in the form of a single $25 million Export-Import Bank loan.

[11]Rouhallah K. Ramazani, *Iran's Foreign Policy, 1941-73* (Charlottesville: University Press of Virginia, 1975), p. 383.

[12]In 1955, responding to anti-trust pressures at home, each of the five majors in the consortium surrendered a one per cent share to a group of eight U.S. "independents." See Shoshana Klebanoff, *Middle East Oil and U.S. Foreign Policy* (New York: Praeger, 1974), p. 96.

[13]Annual oil revenues increased from less than $10 million in 1954 to some $600 million by 1966.

[14]*U.S. Department of State Bulletin*, March 31, 1975, pp. 402-04.

[15]*Annual Statistical Review*, Petroleum Industry Statistics, 1965-74, Statistics Department, American Petroleum Institute, Washington, D.C., May 1975, pp. 10-13.

[16]*U.S. Department of State Bulletin*, December 15, 1975, p. 863.

[17]Ramazani, *Iran's Foreign Policy, 1941-73*, p. 392.

[18]R. M. Burrell, *The Persian Gulf* (New York: The Library Press, 1972), p. 25.

[19]See Ralph Joseph, "Will Iran Diversify its Arms Supplies?" *The Middle East*, No. 24 (October 1976), pp. 18-20.

[20]*Yearbook of International Trade Statistics*, 1974, Volume I, Trade by Country, p. 450.

[21]*The Middle East*, No. 17 (March 1976), p. 109.

[22]Iranian military officers began to receive training in the U.S. as early as 1950. Three years later an Army coup overthrew the Mossadeq government. One principal U.S. intelligence agent and architect of that coup, Brigadier General H. Norman Schwarzkopf, developed his contacts within the Iranian military while serving in Tehran during World War II as U.S. adviser to the Iranian Gendarmerie.

[23]One U.S. aircraft firm recently found itself pressured by the Iranian government to surrender a "penalty rebate" as punishment for the use of middlemen fees, which remain standard business practice elsewhere in the Middle East. And in Iran today, the U.S. intelligence community finds itself more often doing the bidding of the Shah, as by supporting the Kurdish rebellion in Iraq until 1975, rather than working in any way to undermine Iran's sovereignty.

[24]Acheson, *Present at the Creation*, p. 652.

[25]Iran and the U.S. have not, since 1953, considered using force against one another. Early in 1975, the Secretary of State did mention that force might be used against oil producing states in the event of some actual "strangulation" of the industrial world. But his remarks were aimed at those Arab OPEC nations which recently cut off oil supplies to the West, and not primarily at Iran.

[26]See Robert O. Keohane and Joseph S. Nye, *Power and Interdependence* (Boston: Little Brown and Company, 1977), pp. 165-218.

[27]For a review of this familiar line of argument, see Edward L. Morse, "Crisis Diplomacy, Interdependence, and the Politics of International Economic Relations," in Raymond Tanter and Richard H. Ullman, *Theory and Policy in International Relations* (Princeton: Princeton U. Press, 1972), p. 143; Richard Cooper, "Trade Policy is Foreign Policy," *Foreign Policy* No. 9, Winter 1972-73, p. 18; Seyom Brown, "The Changing Essence of Power," *Foreign Affairs*, January 1973, p. 286; Robert O. Keohane, and Joseph S. Nye, "World Politics and the International Economic System," in C. Fred Bergsten, ed., *The Future of the International Order: An Agenda for Research* (Lexington, Mass.: Lexington Books, D.C. Heath and Co., 1973), p. 118; and Donald J. Puchala and Stuart I. Fagan, "International Politics in the 1970s," *International Organization*, V. 28. No. 2, Spring 1974, p. 263.

[28]A U.S. State Department "policy summary" prepared in September 1950, some months before the nationalization, states that "Both the U.S. and U.K. Governments believe it important that AIOC comply with the (Iranian) request." AIOC thus behaved as a genuine non-state actor, in resisting even its own government. This despite the fact that a controlling share in the company had been held by the British government since before World War I, and despite the prerogative of the government to appoint two AIOC directors. The Chairman of AIOC, Sir William

Fraser, preferred to manage the affairs of the company at a distance from Whitehall. Government officials were glad to accept the profits while being told as little as possible about company affairs. See U.S. Congress, Senate, Committee on Foreign Relations, Subcommittee on Multinational Corporations, *The International Petroleum Cartel, the Iranian Consortium and U.S. National Security,* Washington, D.C.: Government Printing Office, 1974, Part 7, p. 126.

[29]Klebanoff, *Middle East Oil and U.S. Foreign Policy,* p. 28.

[30]See L. P. Ellwell-Sutton, *Persian Oil: A Study in Power Politics* (London: Laurence and Wishart, 1955), p. 305.

[31]Because of excess production capacity in Saudi Arabia and Kuwait, total Middle East oil production could easily be maintained and even increased in 1952, without Iran. AIOC maintained its ordinary rate of annual dividend throughout the Iranian crisis, and in 1952 even offered shareholders an additional 5 per cent cash bonus. A rumor even circulated in Tehran at the time that the nationalization had been planned by AIOC, as a moneymaking venture, with Mossadeq as the company's witting or unwitting agent. See Ellwell-Sutton, *Persian Oil: A Study in Power Politics,* pp. 302-06.

[32]U.S. Congress, Senate, Committee on Foreign Relations, *The International Petroleum Cartel,* Part 7, pp. 270-71.

[33]Anthony Sampson, *The Seven Sisters* (New York: Viking, 1975), p. 216; and James E. Akins, "The Oil Crisis: This Time the Wolf is Here," *Foreign Affairs* (April, 1973), p. 472; and for a dissenting view, V.H. Oppenheim, "The Past: We Pushed Them," *Foreign Policy,* 25 (Winter 1976-77), p. 27.

[34]Akins, "The Oil Crisis," p. 473.

[35]Keohane and Nye, *Power and Interdependence,* p. 192.

[36]Robert O. Keohane, "The Big Influence of Small Allies," *Foreign Policy,* 2 (Spring 1971), p. 170.

[37]Leonard Mosley, *Power Play: Oil in the Middle East* (Baltimore: Penguin Books. 1973), p. 212, and Benjamin Shwadran, *The Middle*

East, Oil, and the Great Powers, 1959 (New York: Council for Middle Eastern Affairs Press, 1959), p. 142.

[38]See Mosley, *Power Play: Oil in the Middle East*, p. 223.

[39]*New York Times*, February 12, 1959, p. 1.

[40]U.S. Congress, Senate, Committee on Foreign Relations, Subcommittee on Near East and South Asian Affairs, *Arms Sales to Near East and South Asian Countries*, 90th Congress, 1st Session, June 22, 1967, Washington, D.C.: Government Printing Office, p. 5.

[41]*Business Week*, November 17, 1975, p. 56.

[42]*Department of State Bulletin*, December 15, 1975, p. 863.

[43]Shahram Chubin and Sepehr Zabih, *The Foreign Relations of Iran* (Berkeley: University of California Press, 1974), p. 124.

[44]*Department of State Bulletin*, May 1975, p. 826.

[45]John Osborne, "Bowing to OPEC," *New Republic*, July 19, 1975, p. 13. By another account, President Ford did mention the impending price increase, and asked for a delay. But the sympathetic quality of U.S. policy toward Iran on this occasion is not in question. See V.H. Oppenheim, *Foreign Policy*, 25 (Winter 1976-77), pp. 44-45.

[46]Acheson, *Present at the Creation*, p, 868.

[47]*Ibid.*, pp. 646-648. By contrast, Anthony Eden recalls that he "slept happily that night," upon learning of Mossadeq's final collapse. Anthony Eden, *Full Circle* (Boston: Houghton Mifflin, 1960), p. 237.

[48]See Akins, "The Oil Crisis."

[49]*Department of State Bulletin*, March 10, 1975, p. 293.

[50]*Department of State Bulletin*, December 15, 1975, p. 864.

[51]*Department of State Bulletin*, October 14, 1974, pp. 496-503.

[52]The 1976 OPEC pricing conflict, which postdates this research, was largely a reenactment of this 1975 "joint loss" dilemma.

[53]Keohane and Nye, *Power and Interdependence*, p. 209.

[54]By a related line of argument, the use of such issue-linkage tactics might seem doubly appropriate. Without fully developed conditions of "complex interdependence" between the U.S. and Iran, the force of an ongoing transnational and transgovernmental regime process, such as that which discouraged linkage strategies in the U.S.-Canadian case observed by Keohane and Nye, is not so strong. The U.S. "special relationship" with Iran is not so well grounded in any self-sustaining process of reciprocal, multi-channel contact and association. It is thus more fragile, and more reliant upon constant demonstration of its value.

[55]*Department of State Bulletin*, November 25, 1974, p. 726-27.

[56]*Department of State Bulletin*, December 15, 1975, p. 863.

[57]*New York Times*, September 11, 1976, p. 1.

[58]"Middle East Energy," *The Middle East*, No. 25 (November 1976), p. 118, and *New York Times*, November 11, 1976, p. 8.

[59]In June 1977 the Carter administration did announce an initial decision against a future sale of 250 F-18 fighter planes to Iran. But this refusal was based upon the unusual nature of the Iranian request for "co-production" of the F-18, and not upon linkage to other disputes, such as oil or human rights.

[60]Interview with Mohammed Reza Shah, reported in *Boston Globe*, March 15, 1976, p. 9.

[61]See Keohane and Nye, *Power and Interdependence*, p. 214.

[62]*Ibid.*, p. 213.

FROM RIVALRY TO ALLIANCE:
U.S. RELATIONS WITH JAPAN
1920-1971

Eul Y. Park

CONTENTS

FROM RIVALRY TO ALLIANCE:
U.S. RELATIONS WITH JAPAN
1920-1971

Eul Y. Park

1. Introduction

Students of international relations are properly concerned with the relationship between conflict and interdependence. They resist the notion that a simple or direct relationship exists between the two. Instead, they base their judgments upon critical distinctions between different degrees of interdependence, between different levels of conflict, and between the differing interests and perceptions of the parties involved. In *Power and Interdependence*,[1] Keohane and Nye focus not only upon conflict and interdependence, but also upon the process of conflict management, as one determinant of conflict outcome. The Keohane and Nye study of U.S.-Canadian relations was of particular interest because it demonstrated that a "realist's" view of world politics did not capture the reality of postwar relations between these two countries. Relations between the U.S. and Canada were better understood through an alternative view, "complex interdependence," which has been described elsewhere in this volume.

To what extent are postwar U.S.-Canadian relations unique? To answer this important question, Keohane and Nye proposed additional case studies, preferably of U.S. relations with countries which share some important characteristics with Canada, but which otherwise differ from the Canadian example. Japan is an obvious choice, because it shares with Canada the important characteristic of advanced economic standing and extensive trade with the U.S., while at the same time it lacks the common border and the common language which distinguish U.S. relations with Canada. To insure comparability, this study of U.S.-Japanese relations will employ the same research method devised by Keohane and Nye and used in the study of U.S. relations with Canada and Australia. The analysis will focus upon a single universe of cases, diplomatic disputes between the U.S. and Japan which reached the attention of the President of the U.S., over the period 1920-1971. These disputes will be reviewed against a background of important similarities and differences between U.S.-Japanese and U.S.-Canadian relations, both before and after World War II.

2. Japan and Canada: Similarities and Differences

A starting point for this comparison is the very substantial flow of trade between the U.S. and both Canada and Japan. Canada has remained the most important U.S. trading partner throughout the post-war period, but Japan emerged as second in importance to Canada after 1960. Canada's share of U.S. total exports and imports in 1974 was 20 percent and 22 percent, respectively. Japan's share was 11 percent and 12 percent in the same year. U.S. exports to Canada represented 1.4 percent of U.S. GNP in 1974, while exports to Japan represented .8 percent.

But when we turn to a second kind of international economic activity, foreign direct investment, this appearance of similarity between the two cases is considerably diminished. In 1975, Canada's share of the total value of U.S. foreign direct investment was about 31.2 percent, whereas the Japanese share was only 3.3 percent of the total. One major reason for this dramatic difference was the policy of the Japanese government, which placed heavy restriction on foreign direct investment until the early 1970s. As these policies have been modified, the total value of foreign direct investment in Japan has grown substantially and is expected to continue to grow in the future.[2]

Both Canada and Japan are highly industrialized, democratic societies, similar in political and commercial orientation to the U.S. Indeed, both have been U.S. postwar allies. Yet the dissimilarity between these two allies is also striking. First, while Canada and the U.S. share a common cultural tradition, Japan and the U.S. do not. Differences in religion, language, and racial composition have had a significant impact on the U.S.-Japanese relationship in the past. Although that impact may be gradually lessening today, Japan will forever remain culturally more distant than Canada. A second major difference may be found in the area of direct economic and social contact. We have already noted the low level of direct U.S. investment in Japan, compared to Canada. The lower levels of U.S.-Japanese social contact, from travel and communications, are also highly significant. In terms of flows of people, mail, news, and news media, Canada is almost an extension of the U.S. Japan, by these same standards, is still a *foreign* country. In 1974, for example, only 763,000 Japanese visited the U.S., compared to 8.7 million visitors from Canada.[3]

Finally, U.S.-Canadian security relations are much closer than those between the U.S. and Japan. Unlike contiguous Canada, Japan can not take a U.S. security guarantee for granted. Yet Japan devotes a much smaller proportion of her enormous wealth to military preparedness. Japan remains militarily dependent on the U.S., a condition which is in some ways disguised by Japan's efforts to keep U.S. forces at arm's length. Japan does not want large numbers of U.S. forces stationed on her territory, nor does she want nuclear weapons stored in Japan, for fear of provoking her strong neighbors the Soviet Union and China. But her very heavy military reliance upon the U.S., and her desire to see U.S. forces remain in place elsewhere in the Far East, is undiminished.

In sum, transnational and social interaction between Japan and the U.S. is quite limited and quite shallow compared to U.S. relations with Canada. When turning to the history of U.S.-Japanese conflict relations since 1920, we will find further expression of this essential difference. The analysis will begin with a review of U.S.-Japanese conflicts in the interwar period, 1920-1941. Then, following a similar review of postwar conflict relations, a comparison will be made between the two periods, and between U.S.-Japanese and U.S.-Canadian relations overall. In a concluding section, we will discuss changes in the "regime" which has governed U.S.-Japanese relations since World War II, and the likely durability of the U.S.-Japanese alliance in the future.

3. The Interwar Period: 1920-1941

U.S.-Japanese relations in the interwar period were marked by continuing rivalry and suspicion, quite unlike the postwar experience of alliance and cooperation. Yet within this early period of rivalry, we find substantial differences between conflict issues raised in the 1920s and those raised in the 1930s. As indicated in Table 1, major conflicts were far more frequent in the 1930s than in the 1920s. Of all fifteen interwar conflicts, only four arose before 1930. U.S.-Japanese conflicts in the 1930s also proved far more difficult to resolve. Three of the four conflicts in the 1920s were finally resolved by agreement between the two governments. Only two out of eleven conflicts in the 1930s were resolved by direct agreement; all others either persisted, or were resolved by military conflict. Third, conflicts related to China did not reach the presidential agenda in the 1920s. More than half of the 1930s conflicts were related to

TABLE 1

U.S.-JAPANESE CONFLICTS ON PRESIDENTIAL AGENDA: 1920-1941

Primary issue area of conflict	Nation placing conflict on agenda	Conflict outcome closer to objectives of	Conflict Summary
Politico-military	U.S.	U.S.	1. The Renewal of the Anglo-Japanese Treaty, 1920-22. (U.S. successfully opposed intentions of Japan and U.K. to renew the treaty and replaced it with the Washington Treaty system.)
Diplomatic	U.S.	U.S.	2. The Yap Island Issue, 1921-22. (U.S. opposed Japanese exclusive jurisdiction over the island, which she received from Germany as a part of postwar settlements. Japan yielded despite the weak ground of the U.S. claim.)
Socio-economic	Japan	U.S.	3. The Japanese Immigration Issue, 1920-24. (Japan repeatedly protested U.S. discrimination against Japanese immigrants. However, total exclusion of the Japanese was result of 1924 Immigration Act.)
Politico-military	Japan	U.S.	4. Renewal of the Naval Treaty, 1929-1930. (U.S. successfully opposed Japan's request to change the naval ratio among U.S., U.K., and Japan to the latter's advantage.)
Politico-military	U.S.	Japan	5. The Manchurian Crisis and the Stimson Doctrine, 1932. (U.S. tried to contain Japanese military expansion in Manchuria by announcing Stimson's non-recognition doctrine. Japan ignored U.S.)
Politico-military	Japan	Even	6. Negotiation of a New Naval Treaty, 1934. (Japan requested a new naval ratio in her favor, which was rejected by U.S. and U.K. Japan sent notice to terminate the existing treaty.)

Primary issue area of conflict	Nation placing conflict on agenda	Conflict outcome closer to object- tives of	Conflict Summary
Socio- economic	Japan	Japan	[a]7. Four Power China Consortium and the U.S. Loan to China, 1933-35. (Japan successfully opposed U.S. attempt to make loans to China.)
Socio- economic	U.S.	Japan	[a]8. U.S. Oil Companies in Japan and Manchuria, 1934-37. (U.S. protested in vain against Japan's discriminations against U.S. oil companies in Manchuria and government control of oil companies in Japan.)
Socio- economic	U.S.	U.S.	[a]9. Japan's Voluntary Export Controls, 1934-37. (Japan yielded to U.S. pressure to restrict its export of cotton textiles to Philippines and U.S.)
Joint Resource	U.S.	U.S.	10. The Alaska Fishery Case, 1935-37. (U.S. successfully prevented Japan from fishing salmon near Alaska coast.)
Politico- military	U.S.	Japan	11. Sino-Japanese War, 1937. (U.S. tried to contain Japanese war efforts in China without success.)
Politico- military	U.S.	Japan	[a]12. American Treaty Rights in Occupied China, 1937-41. (U.S. protested repeatedly Japan's restrictions of American treaty rights—commercial, educational, and religious—in the territory occupied by Japan, and destruction of American properties in the war zone. No satisfaction was gained, except in a few cases.)
Socio- economic	Japan	U.S.	[a]13. U.S. Economic Measures against Japan, 1938-41. U.S. adopted embargo, later abrogated the U.S.-Japan Commerce treaty, and finally froze Japanese assets in the U.S., as countermeasures against Japanese military action in China and later in other parts of Asia.)

[a]Transnational organizations significantly involved

Primary issue area of conflict	Nation placing conflict on agenda	Conflict outcome closer to objec- tives of	Conflict Summary
Politico- military	U.S.	Japan	14. Japan's Confrontation Policies, 1940-41. (Japan joined the tripartite treaty in 1940, and later moved its forces to South East Asia, ignoring repeated American warnings and Roosevelt's neutralization proposal.)
Politico- military	Japan	U.S.	15. Final U.S.-Japan Negotiations, 1941. (Final negotiations to prevent a war between the U.S. and Japan failed, as the U.S. held to its rigid position.)

China. Despite these differences, rivalry was the key note in U.S.-Japanese relations throughout the interwar period. To understand the strength and the continuity of this rivalry it is first necessary to summarize U.S.-Japanese relations in a wider perspective.

The Setting

When the U.S. emerged as a Pacific power at the turn of the century, it found itself a latecomer to the struggle for influence in China. Its announced "open door" policy, nominally designed to preserve the integrity of China, was in fact a direct challenge to Japan's special rights the privileges there. Japan, through a series of wars, first against China (1895) and later against Russia (1905), as well as through understandings with other powers, such as the Anglo-Japanese alliance treaty (1902), established a dominant position throughout the Far East. By 1910, Japan had expanded into Taiwan, Korea, and South Manchuria (through control of the South Manchurian railway), and had become a major naval power in the Pacific. During this period the U.S. and Japan came to regard one another as potential enemies.

During World War I, the U.S. and Japan briefly fought as allies, and the conclusion of the war brought Japan an unexpected bounty of foreign exchange reserves and former German territories in the Pacific. Japan concluded from this experience that a policy of cooperation with the U.S. might produce peaceful expansion through trade, capital imports, and immigration. This seemed less costly and more attractive than the alternative of traditional military imperialism. This decision did mean acceptance of a Pacific security regime, based upon the Washington Treaty system, largely established and maintained by the West.[4]

The fact that the U.S. and Japan did not experience frequent or serious conflict in the 1920s reflects this acquiescent posture on the part of Japan. But this interlude of relative cooperation did not change either power's perception of the other as a potential adversary. Ultimately, the Washington Treaty system was not to survive these mutual suspicions.

The U.S. Immigration Act of 1924, which excluded new Japanese immigrants from the U.S. completely, was one early indication for Japan that peaceful expansion and growth through a relatively free movement of capital and goods, might be an illusion. But a more direct challenge to these early hopes came from China itself. A Kuomintang drive to unify China, led by Chiang Kai-shek, threatened Japanese interests in Manchuria. In 1931 the Japanese Kwantung Army occupied Manchuria, and in 1932 the Japanese government established a puppet regime to make permanent its expanded influence.[5]

The U.S. wished to preserve the status quo in the Far East and the Pacific, under the Washington Treaty system, and vainly tried to contain these Japanese military actions in China. Owing to the visible reluctance of U.S. leaders to consider any kind of direct action, these efforts proved a failure.[6] The U.S. merely issued a declaration of non-approval of Japan's policies in China. This policy of "passive non-approval" persisted even after the outbreak of the Sino-Japanese war in 1937, and ended only with Japan's ultimate decision to join the Axis powers in 1940.

When we search for patterns of conflict formation during this interwar period, we note two salient features. First, most interwar disputes (eight out of fifteen) were politico-military in character. The dominance of politico-military issues is further suggested by the fact that two of the five economic issues—those concerning loans to China and economic measures against Japan—had strong politico-military connotations. Yet among the most interesting of these interwar conflicts were those that dealt primarily with economic matters, as the U.S. government sought to defend and protect the endangered interests of far-flung American business operations, such as oil, textiles, and the fishing industry. These interwar economic conflicts are instructive regarding the role played by domestic and transnational actors in U.S.-Japanese relations.

Economic Conflict and U.S. Domestic Industries

Three very different industry groups were the object of conflict between the U.S. and Japan during this period: the textile industry, the fishing industry, and the oil industry.

Until the 1930s, Japan's exports to the U.S. consisted mostly of raw silk and silk fabrics. However, the rapid decrease in silk prices between 1925 and 1931, together with devaluation of the yen in 1931, eventually altered the content of Japan's exports to the U.S. Japan began to export consumer goods, such as cotton textiles, toys, canned fish, glassware, and potteries.[7]

Japanese cotton textile exports had begun their dramatic increase some years before, when shipments from Europe were interrupted by World War I. But these early exports were destined primarily for Japan's colonies, for China, and for South East Asia. Only in the early 1930s did U.S. manufacturers begin to feel the impact of Japanese competition, first in the Philippines, but later in the U.S. domestic market as well. Japan's cotton textile exports grew very rapidly: in 1934, Japan exported 18 million yards to the U.S.; in 1935, 48 million; and in 1936, 73 million. The protectionist response was swift and sure.[8] The National Federation of Textiles, together with other industry organizations, appealed to various government agencies, and to the Congress in 1934, as Congress was debating the Reciprocal Trade Agreements Act. The plight of the textile industry generated such wide concern that President Roosevelt ordered a Cabinet task force to investigate the issue.[9] Considerable pressure was then exerted on the Japanese by the State Department and the Tariff Commission.[10] As a consequence, Japan agreed in 1935 and again in 1937 to restrict exports voluntarily.

The Pacific fishing industry was a second group which felt the danger of Japanese competition. Active lobbying efforts by members of Congress from West Coast states brought this issue to the attention of President Roosevelt.[11] The fishing industry itself maintained leverage with the President by threatening to stage a boycott of all Japanese goods and shipping on the West Coast in cooperation with the longshoremen. Japan's fishing fleets had yet to begin large-scale operations in the traditional salmon fishing grounds off the Alaska coast; the U.S. fishing industry merely wanted to press Japan for a written promise not to do so. This preemptive strategy was a success, as Japan yielded once again.

A third and more complicated interwar economic conflict between the U.S. and Japan involved the protection of U.S. oil companies in Manchuria and Japan. In 1934, Manchukuo, the Japanese-controlled state in Manchuria, monopolized the petroleum industry. In the same year Japan passed a Petroleum Industry Law aimed at stronger government controls of the industry in Japan itself.[12] This law allowed the Japanese government to determine industry import quotas, prices, and stockpile requirements. The Standard Vacuum Oil Company (Stanvac), the largest company operating in Japan and Manchuria, sought to enlist U.S. government support to fight the monopoly in Manchuria and the stiffer regulations in Japan. Stanvac and Shell were contemplating an embargo on crude oil shipments to Japan to force the Japanese government to loosen its control, but they feared that American independent oil companies would quickly replace them as suppliers to Japan and Manchuria. Therefore, Stanvac sought assistance from the U.S. government, which could control the independent oil companies through its powers to regulate exports. Joseph C. Grew, the U.S. Ambassador to Japan, endorsed this plan, but the State Department itself was unwilling to join in such a scheme, fearing the damage which would be done to relations between the two countries. Hence the U.S. limited its actions to an unsuccessful formal protest against the Japanese controls.

These three cases suggest that the U.S. government was responsive to claims from domestic industries, and successful in gaining satisfaction for those industries on two occasions, but that its response was ultimately limited by its regard for diplomatic above commercial interests. In the economic as well as in the politico-military area, the typical U.S. response to Japanese expansion was "non-provocative non-approval."

Conflict Management: Linkage

Once a conflict issue is raised, its resolution may depend upon the bargaining strategy selected by the parties involved. One possible strategy is to draw a link between two separate conflict issues, that is, to adopt a strategy of *quid pro quo*. The Keohane and Nye study of U.S.-Canadian and U.S.-Australian relations shows that such linkage strategies were indeed prevalent in U.S. foreign policy during the period before World War II, but seldom apparent during the postwar period. U.S.-Japanese relations depart from this pattern somewhat. Throughout most of the interwar period, up until the outbreak of the Sino-Japanese war of 1937, linkage was scarcely used by either party.[13] There are several reasons for that.

First, the nature of the issues raised between the U.S. and Japan made direct linkages more difficult to establish. Many of the issues, including those relating to the naval treaties and to China, were not strictly bilateral issues. Other powers, particularly Great Britain, played a salient role. The presence of influential third parties made linkage more difficult to manage. Second, certain issues were far more important to one country than to the other, so that not even threats of linkage would make concessions attractive. Issues related to China, for example, were absolutely critical to Japan. The Japanese government was not prepared to barter away its interests in China in return for benefits on any other matter. Finally, neither party felt that it held a dominant military position during the interwar period, and both knew that linkage strategies could not be adopted without risking further deterioration in their relations. Both opted for a strategy of risk aversion.[14] Only very late during the interwar period did the U.S. become determined to contain Japanese military expansion even at the risk of going to war. Only then did the U.S. resort to a variety of economic sanctions against Japan, linking these sanctions to differences on other issues. With the exception of this immediate prewar period, issue linkage was the exception in interwar conflict relations, not the rule.

Transnational Organizations

Transnational actors, such as multinational corporations, did play an important role in stimulating interwar conflict between the U.S. and Canada. Moreover, as an alternative source of leverage and contact, they were sometimes useful to Canada in the conflict management process. But the role of transnational organizations in U.S.-Japanese relations during the interwar period was comparatively insignificant.

Transnational actors were directly involved in provoking only two interwar conflicts between the U.S. and Japan: the oil monopoly issue, already discussed, and the treaty rights conflict in China, following the outbreak of the Sino-Japanese War in 1937. In both cases American transnational organizations appealed to the State Department for assistance. In neither case did they receive satisfaction. As noted earlier, Stanvac received only a limited measure of U.S. government support in its fight against Japanese control. The company was forced to adjust as best it could to Japanese terms for continuing business activities in Manchuria and Japan. The second case, concerning Japan's violation of American treaty rights in China, arose in response to appeals for protection by U.S. business and missionary interests. U.S. protests were made on behalf of these interests, but they proved to be largely ineffective. Of the fifteen interwar conflicts noted in this study, these were the only two prompted by transnational organizational activity. Two other cases, the China consortium loan issue, and the U.S. embargo against Japan, did involve transnational organizations, but only as passive instruments of official policy. To explain this low salience of transnational activity it is necessary to recall the commercial environment in which such private groups operated.

During the interwar period the U.S. and Japan were major trading partners with each other. Japan was the third largest foreign market for U.S. exports, behind Canada and the United Kingdom, receiving five to seven percent of total U.S. exports. Specifically, Japan was an important market for American raw cotton, petroleum, and other raw materials and producer goods. U.S. investment in Japan was in great measure related to this large export trade with the region. Also, as a source of U.S. imports, Japan ranked second, following Canada, with a market share ranging from seven to ten percent. This trade interdependence was no less significant from Japan's perspective. The U.S. was Japan's most important market for both imports and exports outside of Asia.

But these patterns of commercial interaction were not fully satisfactory to Japan. As noted, most U.S. direct investment in Japan was designed to facilitate the sale and distribution of goods from America, rather than manufacturing in Japan. General Electric, I.T.T., B.F. Goodrich, and Libbey-Owens did establish manufacturing plants in Japan, and General Motors and Ford did maintain auto assembly plants in Japan during the interwar period. But Stanvac, Texas Oil, U.S. Steel, Singer, Eastman Kodak, and others invested in Japan primarily to help promote product sales. Japan's policy toward such multinational firms was far from friendly in the mid to late 1930s. The unstable international economic environment, together with Japan's new concern with national defense, led the government to adopt policies to lessen Japan's dependence on foreign business firms. Japan sought to develop "national industries," particularly is such important areas as automobiles and petroleum.

We have noted already the unsuccessful efforts by Stanvac to resist the Japanese government's control policies. U.S. car makers experienced similar difficulties and met similar frustration. Until the early 1930s, the automobile industry in Japan had been completely dominated by subsidiaries of G.M. and Ford, which imported knockdown models for local assembly. But in 1936 the Japanese government announced an Automobile Industry Law aimed at developing a competitive national industry. Automobile manufacturing now required a government license which would be given only to firms with a majority share held by Japanese citizens. Foreign companies were forced to observe rigid annual production quotas.

Ford and G.M. hoped at first to continue manufacturing cars in Japan under these new national controls. But in view of worsening relations between the two governments they finally gave up the idea. Other American firms, particularly those affected by Japanese military actions in China, also became resigned to their fate. They did not petition their home government for retaliation against Japan because they did not wish to jeopardize the much larger business interests which they maintained in Japan itself. Some even hoped that business opportunities in China would expand under Japanese rule.

So the attitude of those transnational actors which dealt with Japanese trade and investment was generally in accord with official U.S. policy: non-provocation. American business leaders trusted that their interests would be best served if the U.S. could only maintain good relations with Japan.

It is of interest that this passive role adopted by American multinationals was mirrored in the behavior of business leaders in Japan. Japanese businessmen did *not* support military policies in China in the early 1930s, advocating instead close Japanese cooperation with the U.S. and the United Kingdom. But the Japanese military and the Japanese public considered such views to be symptomatic of undue foreign influence in the Japanese economy. When, after 1937, the military tightened its control over the government, Japanese business leaders found that they had no choice but to support government policy.

Transnational actors did at least provide additional channels of contact between the U.S. and Japan. Perhaps the most significant of these was through J.P. Morgan and Co., and its partner Thomas W. Lamont. The Morgan Company was a financial agent of the Japanese government in the U.S. in the early 1930s, and was instrumental in selling Japanese long-term securities and providing large loans. Lamont had close friends in high government positions not only in the U.S. and Japan, but also in China. Prior to 1937 he was generally tolerant of Japanese actions in China, but after the outbreak of the Sino-Japanese war he repeatedly warned his Japanese friends that the war against China would lead to a disastrous military confrontation with the U.S. Once again, both the direction and the timing of his private views ran quite parallel to the evolution of official U.S. policy.

In sum, an atmosphere of increasing U.S.-Japanese rivalry, together with parallel views toward Japan held by private as well as official actors, reduced the independent role of U.S.-based transnational actors during the interwar period. And in Japan, private actors were given little leeway by their military government. In such an environment, interdependence alone is not enough to reduce the role of sovereign nation states.

Explaining Conflict Outcome

U.S.-Japanese conflicts were resolved to U.S. satisfaction more in the 1920s than in the 1930s. In the 1920s, all four conflicts were settled to the advantage of the U.S. But in the 1930s, the U.S. was able to prevail in only four of eleven disputes. Even when economic issues are excluded, conflicts in the 1930s were resolved twice as often in favor of Japan.

Early U.S. success in controlling conflict outcome can best be explained as the result of Japan's policy of cooperation, under the prevailing regime of the Washington Treaty system. It was when this policy began to change, in the 1930s, that Japan began to prevail in an increasing number of diplomatic disputes with the U.S. During the 1930s, neither nation enjoyed clear military preponderance in the Pacific, but Japan felt a much stronger sense of "jurisdiction" over Asian mainland disputes, while the U.S. felt a natural sense of jurisdiction over matters affecting its domestic industries. Japan's overall success in conflict outcome in the 1930s reflects the very large number of China-related politico-military issues on the agenda, and the rather small number of issues affecting U.S. domestic industries.

To summarize, interwar relations between the U.S. and Japan were marked by increasing rivalry and incompatibility. Under such circumstances, it is to be expected that political and military considerations will dominate the diplomatic agenda, and that transnational and other non-governmental actors will not play a significant role in interstate relations. In short, U.S.-Japanese relations before Pearl Harbor were governed by a highly traditional regime of rivalry and security conflict. This regime brought about a total war, total defeat for Japan, and only then a possible evolution toward "complex interdependence."

4. The Postwar Period: 1952-71

Japan's military defeat in World War II brought its imperial ambitions to an unceremonious conclusion. In the process, the war also settled Japan's outstanding disputes with the U.S. Following seven years of military occupation, Japan was offered a new relationship with the U.S., that of a weak and dependent ally.

Until the end of the 1950s Japan remained heavily dependent upon the U.S., for economic assistance as well as for security protection. When, in the 1960s, Japan's complete economic revival led her to become the third largest economic power in the world, her relations with the U.S. began to reflect a more assertive stance. Dependence had been replaced by interdependence. In fact, by the late 1960s and early 1970s, Japan's success at playing the game of interdependence with the U.S. prompted a series of major conflicts, and several significant regime adjustments. Yet overall, Japan's security dependence on the U.S. had changed very little.

U.S.-Japanese relations in the postwar period were marked by a dramatic increase in commercial contact. Under the protection of a security alliance, these contacts grew rapidly to surpass those of the prewar period. In 1953, Japan's share of total U.S. exports and imports stood at 5.6 percent and 2.4 percent. By 1974, this share had increased to 10 percent and 16 percent, and Japan ranked second only to Canada among major U.S. trading partners. Meanwhile, the U.S. share of Japan's imports and exports changed from 18.4 percent and 31.5 percent in 1953, to 23.1 percent and 20.4 percent in 1974. America has remained Japan's prinicpal trading partner throughout the entire postwar period. Capital movements in the form of direct investment did not grow as rapidly as trade in the postwar period, due to Japan's persistent efforts to restrict foreign ownership. But with a recent modification of Japan's restrictive policies, U.S. investment increased. U.S. direct investment in Japan by the end of 1974 reached $3.3 billion, about 3.3 percent of the U.S. overseas total.[15]

This postwar increase in U.S.-Japanese commerce has had some direct spill-over effects on other kinds of transnational contact, specifically travel. In 1974, 763,000 Japanese visited the U.S., while the number of American visitors to Japan also increased substantially. The question must be asked, then, how this postwar growth in economic interdependence, alongside an unusual degree of continuing security dependence, has altered the conduct of U.S.-Japanese conflict relations.

Agenda Formation

During the postwar period, until the late 1960s, it is notable that most

TABLE 2

U.S.-JAPANESE CONFLICTS ON PRESIDENTIAL AGENDA: 1952—1971

Primary issue area of conflict	Nation placing conflict on agenda	Conflict outcome closer to objectives of	Conflict Summary
Diplomatic	U.S.	U.S.	1. The Yoshida Letter Case, 1951-52. (U.S. pressured Japan successfully to send a letter committing Japan not to recognize the People's Republic of China after Japan's independence.)
Politico-military	U.S.	U.S.	2. Strengthening Japan's Self Defense Forces, 1952-57. (U.S. kept requesting Japan to strengthen its forces to play a more active role in defense of Japan and in a regional security system. Japan met U.S. requests at a limited pace.)
Socio-economic	U.S.	U.S.	3. Japan's Voluntary Export Control of Cotton Textiles, 1956-57. (Japan yielded to American pressure to adopt export restrictions.)
Politico-military	Japan	Japan	4. Girard Case, 1957. (U.S. initially opposed the trial of Pfc. Girard in Japanese courts. But later it changed its position and yielded to Japanese request.)
Politico-military	Japan	U.S.	5. Nuclear Test Ban Issue, 1957-58. (Japan requested that the U.S. stop testing nuclear weapons, without success.)
Politico-military	Japan	Japan	6. Revision of the U.S.-Japan Security Treaty, 1955-60. (Japan repeatedly requested U.S. to agree on revision of the treaty, to place relations on a more equal and mutual basis. U.S. finally agreed.)
Joint Resource	Japan	U.S.	7. The North Pacific Fishery Convention, 1963-65. (Japan wanted to revise the 1953 fishery treaty which restricted Japanese fishing of salmon and halibut. The U.S. did not yield.)

Primary issue area of conflict	Nation placing conflict on agenda	Conflict outcome closer to objectives of	Conflict Summary
Socio-economic	Japan	Japan	8. The Interest Equalization Tax, 1963-65. (The U.S. initially did not agree to Japan's request to exempt her from the law. In 1965 U.S. gave Japan a limited exemption, $100 million a year.)
Socio-economic	Japan	Japan	[a]9. Amendment of the U.S.-Japan Aviation Treaty, 1960-65. (U.S. repeatedly refused Japan's request to allow Japan Air Lines to fly to New York. In 1965 U.S. finally agreed in exchange for U.S. landing rights in Osaka and additional flying rights beyond Tokyo.)
Socio-economic	U.S.	Japan	10. The U.S. Balance of Payments Issue, 1968. (U.S. wanted an arrangement similar to that between U.S. and W. Germany, to help U.S. balance of payments position. Japan showed only a limited response.)
Diplomatic	Japan	Japan	11. The Return of Okinawa, 1965-69. (U.S. finally responded favorably in 1969 to Japan's request to return the island on the Japanese terms.)
Socio-economic	U.S.	U.S.	[a]12. Japan's Trade Barriers and Trade Balance, 1969-71. (Japan yielded to U.S. pressures to expedite Japan's trade liberalization and to reduce its trade surplus.)
Socio-economic	U.S.	U.S.	[a]13. Japan's Liberalization of Foreign Direct Investment, 1965-71. (Japan seriously began to liberalize direct investment restrictions in the early 1970s, under heavy pressure from the U.S.)
Socio-economic	U.S.	U.S.	[a]14. Japan's Voluntary Control of Man-made Textile Exports, 1969-71. (Despite Japan's strong resistance to the U.S. request to adopt restriction measures, Japan finally yielded under heavy U.S. pressure.)

[a]Transnational organizations significantly involved

Primary issue area of conflict	Nation placing conflict on agenda	Conflict outcome closer to objectives of	Conflict Summary
Socio-economic	U.S.	U.S.	15. The U.S. New Economic Policy, 1971. (Japan reversed its initial position to maintain the old exchange rate with the dollar under U.S. pressure and agreed to appreciate the yen.)

conflict issues were placed on the agenda by Japan. Note from Table 2 that Japan raised the first conflict issue in seven of the ten postwar conflicts raised before 1968. This pattern of agenda formation is in keeping with a general expectation that a weaker alliance member will place issues on the diplomatic agenda to counter unilateral policy actions taken by the stronger member. But Japan had an additional reason to initiate "interstate requests" during the first part of this postwar period. Japan was naturally eager, after the occupation ended, and as its economy revived, to alter the alliance relationship to reflect at least nominal equality. The revision of the U.S.-Japanese security treaty, the fishery conflict, the aviation treaty, and the Okinawa issue, all originated in Japan's desire to correct the one-sided nature of earlier agreements between the two countries, agreements which had been concluded when Japan was in a helplessly dependent state.

In the late 1960s the tables were turned. Every single conflict issue raised after 1968 was placed on the agenda by U.S. request. This suggests that Japan had been more than successful in its earlier efforts to redress the balance of the relationship. The U.S., after 1968, was struggling to recover advantages from the relationship which it, as the dominant military partner, felt it still deserved. Japanese trade barriers, the growing Japanese trade surplus, restrictions on U.S. direct investment, and the undervalued yen, all became objects of U.S. attack in the late 1960s.[16]

Table 2 also indicates that in the postwar era all politico-military conflicts took place in the 1950s. After the 1960 security treaty revision, politico-military issues were not raised to the level of major disputes. This disappearance of politico-military conflict did not mean that security issues had ceased to matter to the parties in the relationship. Rather, it indicated that a successful adjustment had been made and that most of their politico-military interests were highly compatible. Where those interests were not entirely compatible, as with the Vietnam issue, Japan was reluctant to provoke a major conflict with the U.S. in simple recognition of the fact that it could not hope to prevail. Differences over Chinese representation in the U.N. and over U.S. military bases in Japan were also held back from the formal diplomatic agenda by Japan, even though they were prominent in Japanese domestic political debate. Japan knew that her ability to influence U.S. security policy was limited; the decision was made to focus attention on those issue areas where some reward might follow.

Conflict Management: Linkage

As in the case of U.S. relations with Canada and Australia, linkage among conflict issues was not considered a normal bargaining strategy under the alliance regime which governed postwar relations with Japan. Nevertheless, the U.S. did resort to linkage on two occasions.

First, the U.S. desire that Japan strengthen its armed forces was linked to the Japanese desire for a security treaty revision. To obtain the treaty revision, Japan was being asked to contribute more to Asian security by investing more in defense. Ever since the original security treaty had been signed, in 1952, Japanese political leaders had been eager to remove those provisions which allowed free movement of U.S. troops in and out of Japan without prior consultation. But this sort of treaty revision was rejected by Secretary of State John Foster Dulles in 1955. He made it clear that until Japan was ready to play a more active role in defending itself by strengthening Japanese self-defense forces, the U.S. would not consider revision of the security treaty. This U.S. linkage effort eventually failed. Over the next five years, Japan was able to bargain down the size of the demanded force increase. A new security treaty was signed in 1960, resolving this conflict to the relative advantage of Japan.

A second and more celebrated instance of linkage occurred in 1969, when President Nixon responded to domestic political demands that he provide protection for the U.S. textile industry in the face of Japanese imports. Prime Minister Sato was anxious at the time to restore complete Japanese control over the island of Okinawa.[17] So Nixon decided to link U.S. concessions on Okinawa to Japanese concessions on textiles. Although it had been understood by both parties that the return of Okinawa was to be only a matter of time, the timing of the issue was nonetheless critical to Sato's own political future. Consequently, at a 1969 summit meeting, Sato felt that he had little choice but to accept

Nixon's linkage and to promise textile export restraint. Linkage appeared to be working. The U.S. announced its plans to return Okinawa to Japan by 1972.

But then Japan reneged. Sato did not keep his part of the bargain, if he had ever intended to do so. He was not able to persuade the Japanese textile industry, or even his own bureaucrats, to accept Nixon's export restrictions. So this second postwar attempt on the part of the U.S. to employ issue linkage, much like the first, ended in failure.

Issue Hierarchies, Transgovernmental Coalitions, and Transnational Organizations

Unlike the Canadian example, U.S. postwar relations with Japan were tightly constrained by security concerns. It may be a general trend that the role of military force in the conduct of foreign policy has diminished, but in U.S.-Japanese relations security concerns have far from disappeared. Japan, despite its genuine anxiety over Russian military power and over instability on the Korean peninsula, continues to spend less than 1 percent of its GNP on military programs. Instead it reaffirms its reliance on the U.S. security guarantee. The U.S., for its part, does not ignore the strategic importance of Japan.[18] Thus, when major U.S.-Japanese conflicts develop, such as the textile case or the Okinawa issue, both countries evaluate their position in light of larger security concerns. In this sense, security issues still play a significant role in diplomatic bargaining between the U.S. and Japan, even if the number of security issues on the conflict agenda has decreased.

Also, unlike the case of Canada, "transgovernmental coalitions" seldom form to affect the conduct of postwar conflict relations between the U.S. and Japan. In a few cases, major splits within the two governments did provide possibilities for the formation of transgovernmental coalitions. For example, the State Department disagreed with the position of the White House and the Commerce Department in the textile dispute, and the Department of Defense (Joint Chiefs of Staff) and the State Department were in open disagreement over the reversion of Okinawa. In Japan MITI differed with the Foreign Ministry in the textile case. From differences such as these, the rudiments of some transgovernmental coalitions were formed. The senior staff in the U.S. Embassy in Japan and the Japan desk in the State Department informally allied themselves with the Japanese government in the Okinawa reversion case, against the Joint Chiefs of Staff. And in the textile case, one important transgovernmental contact developed between the Japanese and Representative Wilbur Mills, Chairman of the House Ways and Means Committee. Mills helped to develop Japan's unilateral quota proposal (1971), a compromise which sought to "end run" hardliners in the U.S. Congress, the White House, the Department of Commerce, and the U.S. textile industry.

Overall, such transgovernmental coalitions proved to be of small consequence. They were seldom formed, and once they existed, they seldom met with success. In the Okinawa case, the de facto coalition between the Japan desk in the State Department and the Japanese government may have assisted Japan in securing timely reversion. But the efforts of the Mills-Japan coalition were not successful. President Nixon, who was directing the textile negotiations, did not want Representative Mills, a powerful Congressional leader and a Democrat, to receive credit for resolving this highly politicized dispute. Nor could the President neglect opposition from the textile industry. Because of differences in certain values, cultural tradition, religion, language, race, and customs, actors too easily misperceived the intentions and motivations of potential "coalition partners" in the other country. Such conditions of cultural distance, missing in the Canadian case, were an important inhibiting factor in smooth communication between subgovernmental groups in the U.S. and Japan.[19]

Turning to transnational organizations, their postwar role in U.S.-Japanese relations proved to be passive and limited, once again in contrast to the U.S.-Canadian case. Only four of the fifteen postwar conflicts featured substantial transnational organization involvement, fewer than in the earlier interwar period. U.S.-based multinationals did apply strong pressure on the government to negotiate Japanese trade reform and a liberalization of Japan's foreign direct investment controls. And in the textile case, Donald Kendall, Chairman of Pepsicola and also of the Emergency Committee of American Trade, a private liberal trade advocates group, tried hard to mediate between the two parties. Kendall, who had business interests in Japan, was also a good friend of President Nixon, but his mediation efforts enjoyed little success.[20] This relatively inactive role played by transnational actors in postwar conflict relations with Japan follows closely from the fact that levels of foreign direct investment by multinational corporations were relatively low in Japan, certainly compared with Canada or Western Europe. And again, language differences, customs and cultural traditions, and sheer physical distance, further limited transnational activities between the U.S. and Japan.

Accounting for Patterns of Conflict Outcome

It is finally necessary to explain postwar patterns of U.S.-Japanese conflict outcome. This seems at first a simple task. As seen in Table 2, the U.S. prevailed in nine postwar conflicts, to Japan's six. Adherents of the "realist" school can quickly explain this result by observing that the U.S. as the stronger partner naturally enjoyed an advantage. Looking closely, however, we find a complicating factor. U.S. success in conflict resolution was largely restricted to economic or joint resource issue areas. Here the U.S. prevailed twice as often as Japan. In the politico-military issue area, Japan prevailed as often as the U.S. And the two most important non-economic conflicts, revision of the security treaty and Okinawa reversion, were both resolved in favor of Japan. Such results are not compatible with a simple "realist" view that the strong will prevail when security issues are at stake.

When postwar patterns of conflict outcome are sorted over time, a further complication is observed. In the 1950s the U.S. won four cases to Japan's one. In the 1960s an opposite pattern prevailed, as the U.S. won only one conflict, while Japan was successful in five. And in the early 1970s came a final reversal: all four cases were won by the U.S. To account for this unexpected shifting of patterns of advantage, from the U.S. to Japan, and then back to the U.S., a more sophisticated version of the realist's model of alliance bargaining is required. The stronger power does not always seek to prevail in search of short-run benefits. Stronger powers may instead allow their weaker allies to gain such benefits. Absorbing such "losses" is, in fact, the key to long-term alliance maintenance. For Japan to gain satisfaction on Okinawa reversion, and on security treaty revision, added a great deal to long-run alliance maintenance while taking only a little away from immediate U.S. interests.

Japan's success in the 1960s can best be explained with this U.S. motive in mind. Following the revision of the security treaty in 1960, Japan became a junior partner with the U.S., rather than a totally submissive and dependent client. Japan's revived economic strength, together with this new diplomatic status, encouraged its leaders to correct imbalances which existed in other aspects of its relations with the U.S. The U.S. was willing to indulge this decade of redress, in the 1960s, in the interest of long-term alliance stability. But by the early 1970s, Japan's success had helped to produce the opposite sort of imbalance. The U.S. now felt it necessary to request modification of Japan's trade barrier and investment policies, and revaluation of its currency, appropriate to Japan's new status as a world economic power. To secure these modifications required that the U.S. prevail, once again, in the majority of its diplomatic disputes with Japan.

In sum, postwar U.S.-Japanese relations do not conform precisely to the ideal type defined by Keohane and Nye as "complex interdependence." Nor do they conform precisely to the more traditional standard, described as "realism." Instead, a mix is in evidence. Security issues did not play a prominent role in the postwar relationship, but were always in the background as a critical factor. Multiple-level contacts did certainly develop between the U.S. and Japan in the postwar period, but as we have seen, transnational actors and transgovernmental coalitions played, in all but a few cases, passive roles. On the whole, postwar U.S.-Japanese relations seem to fit almost midway between the Canadian example of complex interdependence and the Australian example of realism.

5. The Future of the U.S.-Japanese Relationship

When there was a sudden increase in the frequency and intensity of U.S.-Japanese conflict, in the late 1960s and early 1970s, many informed observers feared that confrontation had permanently replaced cooperation as the dominant characteristic of U.S. relations with Japan. This supposed change was widely attributed to a relative decline in worldwide U.S. hegemonic power and a new disinclination on the part of the U.S. to bear the burdens of alliance leadership. This pessimistic assessment is, at best, premature. A quick review of changes which have taken place in the past will shed some light on the relative durability of the present U.S.-Japanese relationship.

The most important single change in the basic structure of U.S.-Japanese relations was brought about by nothing less than Japan's unconditional surrender at the conclusion of World War II. Reasons for more subtle changes in the relationship, in the 1930s and 1960s, are more diverse. Throughout the interwar period the basic characteristic of the relationship remained one of "rivalry." Beginning in 1932, the cooperative aspect of this rivalry was replaced by policies of confrontation. The main cause of this change was the breakdown of the relatively stable international order, particularly the demise of an open international economic system, in the early 1930s. Japan's leaders took these external events as a signal to adopt strong and expansive nationalist policies.

The change in the nature of the U.S.-Japanese alliance which took place at the end of the 1950s was even more subtle and more gradual than this change which took place in the early 1930s. In this postwar case, a major casual factor was internal rather than external: the recovery of Japan's relative economic position, and a decision to establish diplomatic objectives worthy of this new-found status. Japan's diplomatic success in the 1960s was further made possible by the unquestioned importance ascribed to that country by Cold War strategists in the U.S. These changes in U.S.-Japanese relations, from near-total dependency to effective interdependence, were completed by the end of the 1960s.

What, then, of the major U.S.-Japanese conflicts which occurred in the early 1970s? For the U.S., the purpose of these conflicts was not "shock," but adjustment. Japan's economic policies were to be weaned from some of their outdated insularity. The passage from dependence to inter- dependence would finally be recognized on both sides. The fact that U.S.-Japanese relations for some time after 1971 were largely free from highly politicized economic conflict seems to confirm the success of this adjustment.

By 1977, of course, further adjustment was required. In that year, as Japan's trade surplus with the U.S. approached $10 billion, the Carter Administration insisted upon new Japanese concessions, chiefly a pledge to stimulate internal growth to build a larger market for imported goods from the U.S. Yet the negotiated concessions of January 1978 were not accompanied on either side by the same tone of bitter conflict which marked the 1971 dispute. Indeed, it seemed that the two governments were anxious to reach a public agreement as quickly as possible, to forestall an escalation of protectionist demands in the U.S. Congress.

Does this mean that U.S.-Japanese relations are gradually evolving to approximate the U.S.-Canadian example of complex interdependence? As noted earlier, in some respects the answer is yes. But overall, U.S.- Japanese relations can never grow to approximate those that have developed between the U.S. and Canada. Economic integration and mutual economic adjustment may continue, as long as the leaders of the two nations continue to hold compatible political views. But a major difference separates the U.S.-Japanese relationship from the U.S.- Canadian example. The latter is a natural alliance, born of physical and cultural proximity and economic complementarity. Alliance relations between the U.S. and Japan are more the product of events: Japan's defeat in World War II, and of the onset of the Cold War. Despite the very large mutual gains to be derived from growing interdependence between the U.S. and Japan, and despite the apparent success in adjusting the relationship to new realities of economic interdependence, Japan's relations with the U.S. still remain contingent upon diplomatic and security calculations. For this reason we must limit our speculation to a short-term or mid-term future. Further evolution of U.S.-Japanese interdependence rests on the continued pursuit of compatible security goals. In this sense, the essentials of realism coexist with aspects of complex interdependence.

NOTES

[1]Robert O. Keohane and Joseph S. Nye, *Power and Interdependence* (Boston: Little Brown, 1977).

[2]Since 1971 under the third (April 1971), fourth (August 1971) and fifth (May 1973) rounds of liberalization, Japan has reduced substantially the number of industries in which foreign direct investment is restricted. According to the U.S. Department of Commerce (The Survey of Current Business), book value of U.S. direct investment in Japan increased from $1,483 million in 1970 to $2,733 million in 1973. For further discussion, see L. Krause and S. Sekiguchi, "Japan and the World Economy" H. Patrick and H. Rosovsky, eds., *Asia's New Giant* (Washington, D.C.: The Brookings Institution, 1976), pp. 444-448.

[3]This figure does not include those Canadians who were admitted less formally, for a short-term visit.

[4]For a well-documented account of this relationship, see Akira Iriye, *Pacific Estrangement* (Cambridge: Harvard University Press, 1972).

[5]Akira Iriye, *After Imperialism* (Cambridge: Harvard University Press, 1965), pp. 13-22. Also, Harold and Margaret Sprout, *Toward a New Order of Sea Power* (Princeton: Princeton University Press, 1946).

[6]For details, see Sadako Ogata, *Defiance in Manchuria: The Making of Japanese Foreign Policy, 1931-1932* (Berkeley: University of California Press, 1964).

[7]Dorothy Borg, *The U.S. and the Far Eastern Crisis of 1933-1938* (Cambridge: Harvard University Press, 1964).

[8]For a discussion of Japan's international economic relations in the interwar period, see Hugh T. Patrick, "The Economic Muddle of the 1920s," in J.W. Morley, ed., *Dilemma of Growth in Prewar Japan* (Princeton: Princeton University Press, 1971).

[9]Mira Wilkins, "The Role of U.S. Business," and H. Nakamura, "The Activities of the Japan Economic Federation," both in D. Borg and S. Okamoto, eds., *Pearl Harbor as History* (New York: Columbia University Press, 1973).

[10]"The President's Special Cabinet Committee on the Cotton Textile Industry" consisted of Secretaries from the State, Commerce, Agriculture, and Labor Departments. See *Foreign Relations of the U.S.* (hereafter cited as *FRUS*), 1935, pp. 988-1011.

[11]*FRUS*, 1935, pp. 1072-1077. Also *FRUS*, 1936, pp. 942-946; *FRUS*, 1937, pp. 748, 759ff.

[12]*FRUS*, 1934, pp. 722, 728ff. Also Mira Wilkins, "The Role of U.S. Business," pp. 362-366.

[13]Even in 1940, the State Department Far Eastern Division opposed any restriction or prohibition on the exportation of petroleum products, fearing Japan's retaliatory move into the Dutch East Indies.

[14]Mira Wilkins, "The Role of U.S. Business," pp. 358-370.

[15]The U.S. did not emphatically request reciprocity on the issues of trade barriers and foreign direct investment control until the late 1960s, and Japan was very slow in removing those controls. For details, see Eul Y. Park, "The Economics and Politics of U.S.-Japan Trade, 1953-1971," Ph.D. Thesis, Harvard University, 1975, Chapter 7.

[16]For a detailed discussion, see I.M. Destler, *Managing an Alliance* (Washington, D.C.: The Brookings Institution, 1976), pp. 12-19, and Martin E. Weinstein, *Japan's Postwar Defense Policy, 1947-1968* (New York: Columbia University Press, 1971).

[17]For an extended discussion of the textile issue, see Park, "The Economics and Politics of U.S.-Japan Trade," pp. 171-207. Also, for the textile issue and the Okinawa issue, Destler, *Managing an Alliance*, pp. 23-45. The textile issue was finally resolved by the U.S. forcing Japan to accept the American proposal, although the linkage strategy itself had been unsuccessful.

[18]Edwin O. Reischauer, "The Broken Dialogue with Japan," *Foreign Affairs*, Vol. 39 (October, 1960), and Zbigniew Brzezinski, *The Fragile Blossom* (New York: Harper and Row, 1972), pp. 111-126.

[19]Destler, *Managing an Alliance*, pp. 143-148.

[20]For example, see the statement of Donald Kendall, Chairman of the Emergency Committee for American Trade, before the Senate Committee on Finance. Senate Committee on Finance, *Hearings on Foreign Trade*, 92nd Congress, 1st Sess., 1971, Part II p. 882.

DEPENDENCE AND CONFLICT:
U.S. RELATIONS WITH MEXICO
1920-1975

Donald L. Wyman

CONTENTS

DEPENDENCE AND CONFLICT:
U.S. RELATIONS WITH MEXICO
1920-1975

Donald L. Wyman

1. Introduction*

In the past, the study of world politics and international conflict mainly concerned the great issues of war and peace, and international power was thought to derive from control over military and economic resources. Because those resources were considered the traditional sources of power it was held that a state with greater control over them would generally be able to get what it wanted in conflicts with states that had less control over them. More recently, however, scholars have observed that many international disputes do not involve armed struggle and that possession of military and economic resources is no guarantee of success in international conflicts. Students of world politics now find it useful to distinguish between power defined as control over resources and power defined as control over conflict outcomes.[1] But why, it may be asked, should a state strong in military and economic resources ever lose a conflict to a state weaker in those resources? What explains outcomes in nonviolent conflicts between states which differ widely in their degree of control over the traditional sources of international power?

The literature of international relations provides at least two kinds of explanations for a weaker state's ability to secure favorable results in

*Several scholars read and commented on earlier versions of this paper. I would like to express my appreciation to Jorge Domínguez, Robert Keohane, Joseph Nye, Jr., Robert Paarlberg, Raymond Vernon, and John Womack, Jr. I am also grateful to Peter Jacobsohn, Editor of Publications at the Center for International Affairs, for many good suggestions and much useful advice.

conflicts with a stronger state. One kind of explanation focuses on the structure of interests in a relationship; it is held, with variations, by scholars who write from what may be termed a realist perspective, and who argue that a major power on occasion is willing to suffer an unfavorable outcome in a specific conflict in order to preserve a relationship or system that is to its overall advantage.

The other kind of explanation emphasizes the political process of conflict bargaining, and it has been most thoroughly articulated by Robert Keohane and Joseph Nye, two political scientists interested in the politics of interdependence. Keohane and Nye have argued that the conditions of what they call complex interdependence may lead to a political process in which a state weaker in military and economic resources may be able to secure a favorable result in a conflict with a state stronger in the traditional sources of power. Relations of complex interdependence between two states are characterized by three conditions: military force is not used or threatened by either government toward the other; the issues about which the two governments disagree vary in substance and there is no consistent hierarchy or priority among them; and finally, multiple channels connect the societies and the governments.[2]

An understanding of the distinctive political process that Keohane and Nye assert is associated with these conditions requires examination of various aspects of conflict relations. Those aspects include the way in which issues become conflicts between the two governments (i.e. the process of politicization), the role of transnational actors and of coalitions between agencies in both governments, the use of retaliation or linkage between issues, and the bargaining position of the conflicting governments, i.e., their intensity and cohesion in pursuit of objectives.

Keohane and Nye examined U.S. conflict relations with Australia and with Canada, and found that while the realist focus on the structure of interests was more appropriate for an understanding of outcomes in the U.S.-Australian case, the conditions of complex interdependence obtained in relations between the United States and Canada. Canadian ability to get favorable results in conflicts with the United States, the authors concluded, was due in part to the political process associated with the conditions of complex interdependence.[3]

This essay extends the Keohane and Nye research by exploring the issues, actors, bargaining processes, and outcomes in presidential-level conflicts between the United States and Mexico from 1920 through 1975. The U.S.-Mexican relationship involves a world power and a developing country, unlike the U.S.-Canadian case, where the mutuality of dependence gave substance to the notion of interdependence. In a study of U.S.-Mexican relations, attention must be given to the *high asymmetry* of the ties of dependence, as well as to the mutuality of the ties. As a case study of how appropriately the notion of complex interdependence applies to conflict relations between states with unequal degrees of control over military and economic resources, the U.S.-Mexican case is much more ambiguous than the U.S.-Canadian relationship. We shall see that some of the conditions of U.S.-Mexican relations match some of the defining characteristics of complex interdependence, while others do not, and we shall argue that U.S.-Mexican relations ought to be understood as relations of dependence, rather than as relations of complex interdependence.

The second section of this essay discusses the extent to which the conditions of U.S.-Mexican relations over time have matched the Keohane and Nye criteria for relations of complex interdependence. The third section analyzes the conflicts and the competing explanations for their outcomes. Section 4 compares U.S. conflict relations with Mexico and with Canada. Section 5 evaluates the contemporary U.S.-Mexican relationship with particular attention to the structures of dependence and to their implications for conflict relations between the two neighboring countries.

2. The Conditions of Dependence

The long history of United States-Mexican relations is summed up in the oft-quoted observation attributed by popular legend to the aged Porfirio Díaz, "Poor Mexico, so far from God and so close to the United States." Mexicans certainly have had many reasons over the years to lament their proximity to the "Colossus of the North," especially in 1848, when Americans marched into their capital and took half of their national territory; in 1914, when President Wilson invaded and occupied the port city of Veracruz in order to teach them to elect honest men; and in 1916, when Black Jack Pershing scoured the northern countryside searching in vain for the elusive Pancho Villa. Today, tourists rather than marines, and Coke signs rather than Old Glory, proclaim the American presence in Mexico, but the people of both countries continue to regard the other with an ambivalence comprising both attraction and suspicion.

Over time, the climate of relations between the two governments has changed. During the decades between the two World Wars, occasional harmony but more frequent tension characterized the climate of relations between the governments of Mexico and the United States. The source of the trouble was evident: American investors trying to protect their property and American officials concerned with international laws regarding foreign investment clashed with triumphant Mexican revolutionaries trying to assert authority over their country's economy. In contrast, relations between the governments after World War II lack the noticeable crises that disturbed prewar relations. The most compelling explanation for the absence of high tension after World War II is the structure of interests, or the ties of mutual dependence, which assured that both governments would seek to control the conflicts between them in order to preserve a relationship from which each stood to benefit.

It is important to emphasize that references in this essay to gains or benefits, either from the relationship in general or from specific conflict outcomes, should not be taken as references to gains in general welfare; we are writing here about governments, not about the majority of people who live under those governments. The Mexican elite may benefit from close ties between Mexico and the United States, but, insofar as income inequality in Mexico is a product of an economic and political system which is strengthened by those close ties, the relationship between Mexico and the United States has not served the interests of the Mexican majority. It is possible to argue, conversely, that poverty would be more widespread in Mexico were it not for the employment created by U.S.-based firms and by the opportunity for Mexicans to cross into the United States in search of work. In any case, the impact of the relationship on the people, rather than on the governments, is an important and complex question not addressed here.

Mexico and the United States have long been connected by ties of history, geography, and commerce, but have they been joined in relations of complex interdependence?

Conditions of U.S.-Mexican Relations and Complex Interdependence

One characteristic of complex interdependence is that military force is not used to settle conflicts. Although the threat or use of military force was important in U.S.-Mexican relations for much of the 19th and early 20th centuries, force has not been a consideration in either the 1920--1940 or the postwar period, when Mexico was neither military threat to nor military ally of the United States, and when the United States government did not use military force against Mexico. This characteristic of complex interdependence clearly is met.

A second characteristic of complex interdependence is an agenda of multiple conflict issues without priority for any one issue. The agenda is the subject of Section 3, but here we note that most conflicts have been over economic issues, and that these economic issues have consistently had priority. The second characteristic of complex interdependence, that the agenda be diverse and without hierarchy, is not met by the conditions of the United States-Mexican relationship, either before or after World War II.

The third characteristic of complex interdependence is multiple channels connecting societies and governments. Contacts between the United States and Mexican societies match this characteristic; those between the governments do not. Consider first the contacts between the societies. Across the 2500 mile common border passes a constant flow of capital and goods, people and ideas, and the international exchanges are as heavy as they are diverse. More about these exchanges later; here suffice it to note that channels of contact between the U.S. and Mexican societies matches the third defining characteristic of complex interdependence.

Consider the contrast in the pattern of contacts between the governments. Although the American Embassy in Mexico City is one of the largest American embassies in the world, U.S.-Mexican governmental contacts during conflicts conform less to the multiple contacts approach that is characteristic of complex interdependence than to the traditional pattern of U.S.-Latin American diplomacy, in which most contacts occur through the representatives and under the auspices of the respective foreign offices. On some issues, primarily technical ones, Mexican officials and their American counterparts from departments other than Relaciones Exteriores and State consult with one another. However, limited evidence suggests that the Mexicans generally work through the State Department and do not frequently deal with the various centers of decision-making authority in the vast American bureaucracy.[4] And, because effective decision-making power in the Mexican government is concentrated in the office of the president, U.S. diplomats have had little incentive to establish direct and frequent working relationships with many of the officials and agencies in the extensive Mexican bureaucracy. With the Mexicans pursuing traditional diplomacy and the Americans directing their attention to the top of the Mexican bureaucracy, governmental relations between the U.S. and Mexico are not characterized by multiple channels, as are relations between the U.S. and more diffusely governed nations, such as Canada. In terms of channels of contact between the governments, U.S.-Mexican relations do not match the third defining characteristic of complex interdependence, either before or after World War II.

In sum, the conditions of United States-Mexican relations in the decades before and after World War II are not very different in terms of how well they meet the defining characteristics of complex interdependence. For both periods the picture is ambiguous. On the one hand, in both periods, two defining characteristics *are not* met: multiple channels do not connect the governments, and the agenda of conflicts is neither diverse nor without consistent priority in the issues of concern. On the other hand, in both periods, some defining characteristics *are* met: military force was not used, and multiple channels of contact bind the societies.

The Structures of Mexican Dependence

Although the conditions of U.S.-Mexican relations match the criteria for relations of complex interdependence in some respects, to perceive the U.S.-Mexican relationship as being like the U.S.-Canadian one would be to miss a dimension crucial to relations between the United States and Mexico: Mexico's economic dependence on the United States. In order to understand this condition of dependence, we must consider in greater detail the international exchanges between the two countries. Complex interdependence directs our attention to the *diversity* of the channels of contact (international exchanges, transnational flows) between the two countries; but, in the U.S.-Mexican case, the flows' *direction*, and their *unequal importance* to the respective countries, are politically more significant features of the relationship than is their diversity. Even though channels of contact between the U.S. and Mexico are multiple, they are highly unequal, and, as sources of influence, they largely favor the United States.

Culture

Consider, for example, the influence of the United States on Mexican culture. It is difficult to measure the impact of attendance at schools in the United States on Mexican officials and businessmen, but we do know that Mexican industrialists travel frequently to the United States to visit fairs and industrial plants, and to participate in conventions and seminars, and that for many of them the United States becomes a cultural model as well as a source of technical information.[5]

Mexican intellectuals are particularly sensitive to the influence of the United States on what Mexicans see and hear: one researcher concluded that 26 of the 49 most popular television programs in Mexico are produced in the United States,[6] and the largest selling magazine in Mexico has long been *Selecciónes,* a Spanish language edition of *Reader's Digest.* Advertising, an important mechanism for the inculcation of values, is dominated by American firms: of the 170 advertising agencies in Mexico, only four are in Mexican hands; the rest, which are controlled by U.S.-based firms, manage 70 per cent of the advertising business that finances Mexican newspapers and radio and television networks.

People: Workers and Tourists

The more important mechanisms of influence are not those of culture, but of economics: the exchanges of persons, capital, and goods. The flow of persons across the border, which is one of the most important kinds of contact between the two countries, has enormous economic and cultural impact, much more so in Mexico than in the United States. The flows are part of the structure of Mexican dependence on the United States: tourism and border transactions have a beneficial effect on Mexico's balance of payments and bring substantial rewards to powerful groups and individuals in Mexico, while legal and illegal migration to the U.S. (to be discussed in more detail in Section 5) and remittances of U.S. earnings by the migrants contribute foreign exchange and bring some relief from distress in rural Mexico.

Although numerous Mexicans come to the United States for business, as tourists, and as consumers, most Mexicans who come to the United States do so to live, or to work for a while and to return eventually to Mexico. Generally, they come without much money or education, and unknown numbers of them enter illegally. Although the continued presence of Mexican consumers and laborers is important to some people and groups in the United States—such as many small entrepreneurs, agribusiness interests, and border chambers of commerce—there are also powerful groups—such as labor unions—who oppose the continued influx of Mexicans.

In Mexico, nobody who argues against the continued inflow of Americans is taken seriously. Americans who go to Mexico do so mostly as tourists (in 1974 they went as tourists to Mexico more than to any other foreign country) and as businessmen or as retirees, and most of them have, and spend, money. Although economists caution that Mexican travel abroad means that net Mexican earnings on tourism are significantly smaller than the figures for gross receipts, most admit that tourism and border transactions have been extremely important sources of foreign exchange in a country with a sharp current account deficit, and that Americans have comprised upwards of 80 percent of postwar tourists to Mexico.[8]

The connection between dependence on American tourists and Mexican foreign policy was revealed most dramatically by the flurry of activity following Mexico's vote in favor of the November 1975 United Nations resolution equating Zionism with racism. Although the Mexican position did not provoke a presidential level conflict, Secretary of State Kissinger wrote Mexican Foreign Secretary Emilio Rabasa expressing the U.S. desire that the resolution be defeated. The retaliation that followed the Mexican government's vote with the Arab bloc came from an unofficial and unexpected source. Angered by the Mexican vote, American Jewish groups organized a boycott of Mexico as a convention and vacation site; within a week, 30,000 hotel reservations were cancelled. Ever sensitive to the economic consequences of a decline in tourism, the Mexican government sent ex-President Miguel Alemán to the United States with an invitation for Jewish leaders to visit Mexico for a talk with President Luis Echeverría, while Rabasa went to Israel to make amends.[9]

The influence exerted in this case by transnational actors should not be exaggerated. The offensive action had already occurred, the Mexicans did not change their vote, and it is questionable whether the boycott even influenced Echeverría's future policy on issues to which American Jews were sensitive: the Mexican government was one of the first to criticize Israel for its raid at Entebbe, Uganda, on July 4, 1976. Nevertheless, the boycott demonstrated the capability of sufficiently organized and aroused groups in the United States to adversely affect the Mexican economy simply by refusing to visit Mexico. Moreover, a decline in tourism to Mexico may occur without specific groups in the United States being aroused over particular Mexican policies: for example, a general belief in the U.S. that turmoil and unrest in Mexico are increasing will induce Americans to stay away from Mexico, as may high diplomatic tension between the two governments. Dependence on American tourists thus induces the Mexican government to minimize conflict with the U.S. government and can be said to be a source of U.S.

influence over Mexican policies. This influence is part of the structure of the unequal relationship and does not have to be explicitly wielded by the United States government.

Capital: Investments, Loans, and Trade

The heart of the structure of dependence, a major source both of conflict and of U.S. influence over Mexican policies, is Mexico's desire for access to American capital and the U.S. market. In order to understand the importance of the transnational flows of capital and goods, it is necessary to consider briefly the development of the postwar political economy in Mexico. Here we will assert that perhaps the most important aspect of U.S.-Mexican relations after World War II, apart from the common border, is the consolidation of power in Mexico by a regime whose first commitment after political stability was to rapid industrial growth through increasing reliance on external financing.

For reasons that are imperfectly understood, the policy preferences of the Ávila Camacho administration, which coincided with World War II, were noticeably different from those of the Cárdenas government of the 1930s. During the war there developed in Mexico a new official concept of the state's role and a new goal for the government: President Lázaro Cárdenas (1934-1940) had described the state as an arbiter among competing class interests and offered as a fitting objective for government the quest for social justice; Ávila Camacho, and most later presidents, said the state was more of an economic regulator in a unified society pursuing its true goal, rapid economic growth.[10] "By the time Ávila Camacho left office late in 1946," wrote one observer of the Mexican scene, "the Cárdenas image of Mexico based upon a contented, semi-industrialized, semi-commercialized peasantry had been obscured by a new image of Mexico—an image of the modern industrial state."[11] Historians debate whether Cárdenas ever envisioned such a Mexico and whether the changes that took place after 1940 were radical departures from the past or merely shifts of emphasis.[12] It is clear, however, that by 1946 the drive toward industrial growth was in full swing.

The initial wartime and postwar growth of manufacturing was the work mostly of Mexican entrepreneurs, but, in the mid- and late 1940s, American firms that had been selling in the Mexican market began to establish assembly and final processing plants in order to avoid rising Mexican tariffs and to benefit from the expanding Mexican economy.[13] In the 1950s, the Mexican government's call for foreign

TABLE 1
Selected Transnational Flows

TRADE

Mexico to and from the U.S.

	Exports		Imports	
	value (in millions of dollars)	as % of Mexican exports	value (in millions of dollars)	as % of Mexican imports
1920	—	—	—	—
1938	125.1	67	63.1	58
1953	367	74	670.9	83
1962	553.3	60	782.5	68.5
1970	838.9	60	1567.5	63
1975	1772	62	4113.3	63

U.S. DIRECT INVESTMENT IN MEXICO

	value (in millions of dollars)	as % of DFI[a] in Mexico	Mexico as % of U.S. world-wide DFI[a]
1920	535	—	16.9
1929	709	—	9.4
1940	357	61.2	5.1
1950	415	68.9	3.5
1960	900	83.2	2.4
1970	1786	85	2.3
1974	2825	—	2.4

[a]Direct Foreign Investment

SOURCES: Leo Gebler, *Mexican Immigration to the United States: The Record and its Implications.* Advance Report No. 2 of the Mexican-American Study Project, Division of Research, Graduate School of Business Administration, University of California, Los Angeles, California, 1966; Lorenzo Meyer, "Cambios Políticos y Dependencia. México

TRADE

U.S. to and from Mexico

Exports		Imports	
value (in millions of dollars)	as % of U.S. exports	value (in millions of dollars)	as % of U.S. imports
208	3	179	3
62	2	49	2.5
436	3	355	3
821	4	578	3.5
1704	4	1219	3
5144	5	3112	3

IMMIGRATION
Mexicans as % of total U.S. immigrants

1920-1924	8.89
1925-1929	15.68
1935-1939	3.21
1940-1944	8.13
1955-1959	15.34
1960-1964	15.35
1968	9.59

en el Siglo XX," *La Política Exterior de México: Realidad y Perspectivas,* Centro de Estudios Internacionales (Mexico: El Colegio de México, 1972); United Nations Statistical Papers, *Direction of Trade;* International Monetary Fund, *Direction of Trade;* U.S. Department of Commerce, Bureau of the Census, *Historical Statistics of the United States* and *Statistical Abstract of the United States;* Mira Wilkins, *The Maturing of Multinational Enterprise: American Business Abroad from 1914 to 1970* (Cambridge, Mass.: Harvard University Press, 1974).

investment became explicit, and, despite ambiguity in the Mexican welcome, the quantity and strategic importance of U.S. direct private investment in Mexico continued to grow.[14] In 1938, U.S. capital accounted for 61.6 percent of total direct foreign (U.S. and non-U.S.) investment in Mexico; two decades later the percentage was 74.4, and by 1972 it had grown to almost 80.[15] More important, the postwar U.S. investment was, and is, located in manufacturing, the economy's most dynamic sector. In 1940, manufacturing claimed only 2.7 percent of total U.S. investment in Mexico; by 1957 it accounted for 45.3 percent, and by 1972 it attracted 69 percent.[16]

Also critical to the well-being of the Mexican economy has been the steady flow of American government grants and loans, which became especially important in the 1950s, when the administration of Adolfo Ruiz Cortines (1952-1958) turned to external financing to support development programs. U.S. government grants and loans provided much of the funds used within Mexico by Nacional Financiera, the government's development bank. Of almost two billion dollars in financial assistance committed to Mexico between 1946 and 1967, approximately 53 percent was in the form of U.S. government grants and loans, and figures for 1976 indicate that approximately three-fourths of Mexico's foreign debt is with U.S. private banks and with multilateral lending agencies such as the World Bank and the International Monetary Fund, in which the U.S. government wields substantial influence.[17]

Finally, proximity to the United States has shaped Mexican trade patterns. The conditions of access to the U.S. market have generated several postwar conflicts between the neighboring countries. We shall discuss the conflicts in greater detail in Section 3; here we note the asymmetry in the importance of the commercial exchange. In recent years, Mexican trade has accounted for approximately four percent of U.S. world commerce, and Mexico has ranked fifth among U.S. export markets. The picture looks very different from the Mexican perspective: since the end of World War II, the United States has provided at least half of Mexico's trade in both directions, and frequently the U.S. took well over 60 percent of Mexican exports and was the source of well over half of its total imports.[18]

Stakes for the United States

The imbalance of influence and resources in the U.S.-Mexican relationship is high, but it is not absolute. Numerous American interests in Mexico assure U.S. sensitivity to Mexican domestic and foreign policies; the U.S. government has strong incentives not to take Mexico for granted at every turn. Specifically, the U.S. government held as policy objectives through much of the Cold War the preservation of political and economic stability in Mexico and the continuation of cooperative alliance behavior on the part of the Mexican government. The American economic stakes in Mexico were substantial, of course, but the U.S. government was also concerned with less tangible but equally important interests. Since World War II, stability in Mexico has been a source of relief to U.S. officials troubled by turmoil, the specter of communist subversion, and the suppression of human rights in the rest of Latin America. In addition, Mexico was a cooperative Cold War political ally: although, as we shall see, the U.S. government was not always pleased with Mexico's votes in the Organization of American States, Mexico did not oppose vital U.S. interests, and it did not criticize U.S. policies outside of the Western Hemisphere.

Relations of Dependence

In the decades after World War II, the governments of the United States and Mexico wanted something from each other, and they both sought to minimize conflict and to maximize cooperation. But Mexico was much the more sensitive party in the relationship, and it was much more vulnerable to the potentially adverse impact of U.S. policies than the U.S. was to any possible effects of Mexican policies. The condition of multiple channels of contact in U.S.-Mexican relations matches a defining characteristic of complex interdependence. But imbalance of economic exchange and more critically, the differing significance of that exchange to the two countries, suggests that the U.S.-Mexican relationship ought to be understood as one of *dependence* more than interdependence.

We are not here arguing for, nor are we attempting to refute, the structural dependency hypothesis that the development of the metropolis (U.S.) requires the continued underdevelopment or exploitation of the periphery (Mexico). We are also not asserting, as would some Mexican intellectuals, that Mexican development strategy after World War II was dictated by fear of a hostile United States reaction to more radical measures: as has been pointed out, the policy preferences of the Mexican ruling coalition after the war would have supported conservatism, even if they had not paralleled those of the United States.[19]

We do argue that Mexican development policies created a situation in which the ruling coalition identified national interests with the availability of external financing and with access to the American economy. The availability and the access, in turn, were seen to depend upon foreign and domestic policies that were acceptable to the U.S. government and/or to the American private sector. The high Mexican sensitivity to anything that adversely affected Mexico's access to foreign capital and markets was due to the postwar Mexican development strategy; the strategy was an outcome of public policy decision-making; public policy outcomes are a product of the particular distribution of power in a country, and they reflect the ends to which that power is used. It is impossible to understand international dependence, then, without understanding the dependent country's internal politics.

Although each government had strong incentives for cooperation with the other, each also responded to pressures that conflicted with the interest in cooperation. The bilateral conflicts that resulted are described below.

3. Conflicts and Outcomes

Presidential level conflicts between the United States and Mexico occurred both in the period between the wars (1920-1940), when relations were often tense, and in the postwar period (1945-1975), when relations were usually calm. We have focused only on the bilateral conflicts that can be shown to have come to the attention of the president of the United States. The seven prewar and fifteen postwar presidential level conflicts are summarized in Table 2 on the following pages.[20]

The indication in Table 2 of the issue area pertinent to each conflict illustrates a constant in the U.S.-Mexican relationship over time: the preponderance of economic conflicts. Between 1920 and 1975, 16 of 22 disputes (72 percent) were about economic issues.[21]

Remarkable is the absence of any military-security conflicts in either period or of any postwar diplomatic disputes. The absence of military conflicts is easier to explain. In both the prewar and the postwar periods Mexico was a military nullity: it did not seriously fear attack from external enemies, and its relatively small armed forces were neither equipped nor expected to participate in combat outside of national territory.[22]

TABLE 2

U.S.-Mexican Conflicts on the U.S. Presidential Agenda: 1920-1975

PREWAR

Primary issue area of conflict	Nation placing conflict on agenda	Conflict outcome closer to objec- tives of	Conflict Summary
Economic	U.S.	Even	1. General Damage Claims, 1900-1941. (The governments could not agree on the method for settling two sets of claims by the citizens of each country against the government of the other. Claims from the revolutionary period (1910-1920) were settled in 1934; general claims from 1860-1910 and agrarian claims after 1927 were settled in a comprehensive agreement in 1941.)
Economic	U.S.	U.S.	2. Petroleum Ownership, 1917-1928. (U.S. protested as "retroactive and confiscatory" various Mexican decrees pertaining to resource ownership and regulation of the oil industry. In 1928, Mexico satisfied the U.S. by changing the offending legislation and decrees.)
Economic	U.S.	Mexico	3. Land Expropriation, 1917-1941. (U.S. protested as "arbitrary and confiscatory" Mexican decrees intended to implement the agrarian reform program. Although land distribution slowed down in the late 1920s because of economic difficulties and low agricultural production, distribution of land increased rapidly during the administration of Lázaro Cárdenas in the 1930s. Mexico made temporary compromises on this issue, but it did not change its agrarian legislation to satisfy the U.S. nor did it meet U.S. demands either promptly to pay for or return expropriated lands.)
Diplomatic	Mexico	Mexico	4. Recognition, 1920-1923. (Mexico gained recognition from the U.S. without complying with U.S. demands for a prior treaty of amity

Primary issue area of conflict	Nation placing conflict on agenda	Conflict outcome closer to objectives of	Conflict Summary
			and commerce, which would have embodied guarantees to owners of property in Mexico. The Mexican government did engage in informal bilateral talks that placated the U.S., but no treaty was concluded and the signed minutes of the talks were not binding.)
Joint Resource	U.S.	Even	5. Water Division, 1928-1944. (Both governments tried to arrive at an agreement to govern water use on the lower Rio Grande and Colorado rivers. Differences over principles and procedures, and disagreements within the United States, prevented conclusion of the treaty until the 1940s.)
Diplomatic	U.S.	U.S.	6. Nicaragua, 1926-1927. (In 1926, Mexico responded favorably to a request from Nicaraguan Liberals to supply them with arms to be used against Nicaraguan Conservatives. The U.S. supported the Conservative faction and requested that Mexico cease its support of the Liberals. When tensions between Mexico and the U.S. were reduced in 1927, Mexico stopped its military support of the Liberals.)
Economic	U.S.	Mexico	7. Oil Expropriation, 1938-1942. (When Mexico expropriated U.S.-owned oil properties, the U.S. government supported the oil firms' demands that Mexico pay "prompt, adequate and effective" compensation. Although the U.S. tried to secure return of the properties, supported compensation estimates proposed by the oil firms, and demanded arbitration, Mexico satisfied none of the U.S. demands. The settlement was much closer to the Mexican estimate of appropriate compensation than it was to that of the oil firms.)

Primary issue area of conflict	Nation placing conflict on agenda	Conflict outcome closer to objectives of	Conflict Summary
			POSTWAR
Economic	Mexico	Even	8. Petroleum Development Loan, 1942-1950. (Mexico requested a U.S. loan for PEMEX, the state oil agency. The U.S. eventually loaned Mexico a much smaller amount than requested, though Mexico did not change its petroleum policy as demanded by the U.S. Although the conflict ended slightly more favorably for Mexico than for the U.S., neither government got what it wanted.)
Economic	U.S.	Even	9. Civil Air Service Agreement, 1945-1957. (Differences over routes and levels of competition prevented an agreement until 1957, when the governments compromised their differences.)
Economic (trade)	U.S.	Mexico	10. Reciprocal Trade Agreement, 1947-1950. (In 1942 Mexico and the U.S. signed an agreement which covered their commercial relations. After Mexico adopted protectionist measures (1947) which were contrary to the spirit of the agreement, the U.S. sought to renegotiate the treaty. Mexico preferred to end it, and when the negotiators failed to agree on new provisions the U.S. reluctantly agreed to the treaty's termination.)
Economic	Mexico	Mexico	11. Migrant Farm Labor, 1948-1951. (Mexico wanted new arrangements to govern contracting of Mexican nationals to work in the U.S.: specifically, it wanted the U.S. government to contract for the workers, rather than to have the hiring done by private firms. In 1951, the U.S. agreed to the "bracero" program, through which Mexican nationals were brought to the U.S. under the U.S. government's auspices.)
Economic	U.S.	U.S.	12. Bracero Program Regulations, 1952-1954. (The U.S. forced Mexico to give up Mexican authority to act unilaterally on several aspects

Primary issue area of conflict	Nation placing conflict on agenda	Conflict outcome closer to objectives of	Conflict Summary
			of the program, including recruitment and transportation of the workers.)
Joint Resource	Mexico	U.S.	13. Coastal Fisheries, 1950-1967. (Mexico wanted U.S. fishermen out of waters it claimed. The U.S. refused to recognize the Mexican claims. A 1967 compromise permitted ships of both nations to fish in coastal waters claimed by the other through 1973. Since 1973, with international organizations tackling the problem of ocean resources, fisheries have not been a presidential level problem between Mexico and the U.S.)
Economic (trade)	Mexico	U.S.	14. Trade Relations, 1950s-present. (Mexico unsuccessfully sought reductions in U.S. restrictions on imports of agricultural commodities and in duties on manufactured imports. Although Mexico has secured occasional victories on specific items, it remains dissatisfied with access to U.S. market.)
Economic (trade)	Mexico	U.S.	15. Cotton Exports, 1950s. (Mexico unsuccessfully protested a U.S. decision to subsidize exports of cotton from U.S. Although a consultation mechanism was established at U.S. initiative, U.S. cotton policy did not satisfy Mexico.)
Economic (trade)	Mexico	U.S.	16. Lead & Zinc Quotas, 1957-1965. (Mexico unsuccessfully protested restrictions on imports of lead and zinc to the U.S.)
Economic (trade)	Mexico	U.S.	17. Sugar Quotas, 1960s. (Mexico fought to prevent reductions in its sugar quota, but reductions were made in 1965.)
Joint Resource	Mexico	Mexico	18. Colorado River Salinity, 1961-73. (Mexico successfully pressed the U.S. to decrease the saline content of water which runs from the United States into Mexico.)

Primary issue area of conflict	Nation placing conflict on agenda	Conflict outcome closer to objectives of	Conflict Summary
			to decrease the saline content of water which runs from the United States into Mexico.)
Competing Sovereignty Claim	Mexico	Mexico	19. "El Chamizal," 1895-1963. (Mexico claimed jurisdiction over an area that had been relocated in the U.S. by a shift in the channel of the Rio Grande River. The issue, largely dormant for 50 years, was raised by Mexico in the 1960s, and, in 1963, the U.S. recognized the Mexican claim.)
Economic	Mexico	Mexico	20. End of Bracero Program, 1963-1964. (In the early 1960s pressure within the U.S. to end the U.S. government-sponsored importation of Mexican workers increased. Mexico did not request that the program be continued, but in 1963 it sought and gained a one-year extension of P.L. 78, the statutory authority for the program.)
Economic	U.S.	U.S.	21. Drug Control, 1960s-. (After unsuccessful efforts to convince Mexico to adopt more strenuous measures to control the movement of drugs through and from Mexico to the U.S., the U.S. government began Operation Intercept, a program of slow and thorough search for drugs at border crossing points. The program quickly and adversely affected tourism and border commerce. Shortly after Intercept began, the two governments announced that it would be replaced with Operation Cooperation, under which the Mexican government would work more closely with U.S. agents fighting the influx of drugs.)
Economic (trade)	Mexico	U.S.	22. Import Surcharge, 1971. (Mexico protested and sought exemption from a 10 percent import surcharge levied by the U.S. as part of the Nixon administration's economic reforms of summer 1971. The U.S. refused to grant Mexico exemption, and removal of the surcharge was not the result of Mexican protests.)

Because Mexico was neither a danger to nor a military ally of the United States, and had no military role to play in world affairs, military-security issues between Mexico and the United States did not arise.

The absence of postwar diplomatic conflicts requires a lengthier explanation. Mexico might have raised diplomatic issues as bargaining chips to give away in exchange for concessions on issues more relevant to its interests. However, the Mexican government did not initiate diplomatic controversies, undoubtedly because such a course seemed more costly than it was worth. For one thing, the Mexican government may have believed that if it had raised diplomatic issues in order to link them to economic issues, the U.S. government might have retaliated by restricting Mexican access to U.S. capital or trade. The imbalance of dependence works in favor of the United States not only within issues (e.g., in terms of trade or investments) but across them as well: Mexico cannot hurt the U.S. diplomatically as badly as the U.S. can damage Mexico economically. For another thing, the political and economic pressures of the national entrepreneurs are an important domestic constraint on the Mexican government. The Mexican economic elite, which was able to exercise much more influence after World War II than before it, undoubtedly would have opposed any government foreign policy that threatened the international exchanges on which postwar economic growth depended.

Dependence as a constraint on Mexican decision-making, and thus as a form of U.S. influence over Mexican policy, operates on two levels, one intentional and explicit, as when the U.S. government in 1975 tied Mexican trade privileges to Mexican non-participation in the Organization of Petroleum Exporting Countries, the other unintentional and implicit in the structure of dependence. The latter is a kind of influence akin to what Jeffrey Hart and Klaus Knorr term "silent power," in which a change in one actor's behavior may result from his anticipation of a change in another actor's behavior, even though the second actor may never have changed his own policy.[23] There may have been occasions when Mexico did not raise diplomatic issues with the U.S. because of its fear of a negative reaction and possibly of retaliation; the U.S. might or might not have reacted negatively, much less retaliated, but if the fear of provoking such a reaction is a constraint on Mexican action, then it is a form of U.S. power over Mexican policy, and it may help to explain the absence of diplomatic conflicts from the agenda. Unfortunately, it is extremely difficult to observe such influence in action, because "silent power operates without any visible attempt to exercise power."[24]

Mexican dependence, whether constraining Mexican actions with or without deliberate effort by the United States, is not the only reason that the agenda contains no postwar diplomatic conflicts. Mexico did oppose U.S. policy toward Guatemala in the 1950s, Cuba and the Dominican Republic in the 1960s, and Chile in the 1970s, but none of these policy differences led to presidential-level conflicts. One reason is that the Mexican government did not turn its opposition to U.S. policy into an anti-American crusade. Another reason is that the Mexican government did not wage campaigns to win other governments to its point of view. A third reason is that the U.S. recognized that a symbolically independent Mexican foreign policy in the Western Hemisphere contributed to political stability and the strength of the regime in Mexico and provided other benefits to broad U.S. foreign policy interests. The combination of the U.S. willingness to concede limited foreign policy independence to Mexico and of Mexican willingness not to seriously challenge vital U.S. political interests in the hemisphere can be seen most clearly in Mexican policy toward Cuba in the 1960s.

When several meetings of the Organization of American States (O.A.S.) and the increasing tension between the U.S. and Cuba forced Mexico to define its policy toward Fidel Castro's government, the López Mateos administration (1958-1964) chose a middle course in form, but a conservative position in substance. It supported the Cuban government's juridical right to be part of the O.A.S. unless the organization's charter were first changed so as to legally permit a charter member's exclusion, but it voted to exclude Cuba from participation in numerous subsidiary agencies, declared that Marxism-Leninism was incompatible with the American system, and, after Cuba was ousted from the O.A.S., maintained correct but cool relations with the Cuban government.[25]

The Cuban question had all the makings of a potential high-level diplomatic conflict between Mexico and the United States. Mexico did not want to have its Cuban policy so obviously dictated by the Yankees, and the United States did not want Mexico to support the Cuban revolutionaries. Through Mexico's adoption of a stance of symbolic but not serious independence from the United States, both governments had their way. Mexican independence fostered the image of a ruling party committed to its revolutionary heritage, an image that was a major source of the Partido Revolucionario Institucional's grip on the Mexican people, and thus of the stability so appreciated by American officials. For the Mexicans, it was a classic case of liberalism abroad in the service of conservatism at home. As noted above, the agreement among policy makers in the U.S. and Mexico to disagree about Cold War policies in the Western Hemisphere prevented high-level diplomatic conflicts over such issues as U.S. policy toward Guatemala, Cuba, and the Dominican Republic.

The Cuban issue also reveals that strong pressures for conflict management work to resolve some diplomatic disagreements at the sub-presidential level, precisely to prevent the escalation of disagreement. These pressures did not always work for economic issues. Although some bilateral economic problems were resolved at lower government levels, many economic issues did reach the attention of the United States president. One reason many economic conflicts got to the president is that economic conflicts call into play the division of powers and the fragmented system of foreign policy decision-making in the U.S. government. Most of the action on political disputes with other countries, especially regarding the Cold War issues in the O.A.S., lay with the State Department; in contrast, economic issues involved governmental and private sector actors with strongly held policy preferences. The State Department, therefore, had less flexibility and authority in the economic conflicts, and it could not have as easily reached a compromise or yielded to Mexican preferences, even had there been an executive desire to do so. Another reason many economic conflicts reached the top of the U.S. political system is that in Mexico's view economic issues were most important. With the force of Mexican concern behind them, the disagreements over economic issues were not as subject to compromise as were disputes over political matters.

Most of the postwar issues were brought to the U.S. president's attention by the Mexican government, primarily through summit meetings, which were probably the only way in which Mexican demands could have commanded such high-level attention in the United States, given Mexico's minor role in the global scheme of postwar U.S. foreign policy. Before World War II, U.S. presidents generally did not meet with their Mexican counterparts, but, since Franklin D. Roosevelt met Manuel Avila Camacho in Monterrey, Mexico, during the war, the American and Mexican chiefs have held meetings, more than half of which were devoted to substantive discussions. The communiqués and reports of these summit meetings provide most of the evidence for U.S. presidential attention to U.S.-Mexican issues.[26]

Pattern of Outcomes

The pattern of outcomes in the presidential-level conflicts was somewhat different in the prewar period than it was in the postwar decades. Of the seven prewar conflicts, the outcomes in three (forty-two percent) favored Mexico, the outcomes in two (twenty-nine percent) favored the U.S., and the outcomes in two were equidistant from the objectives of either government. Of fifteen postwar conflicts, five outcomes (thirty-three percent) were closer to the objectives of Mexico, eight outcomes (fifty-three percent) were closer to the objectives of the U.S., and two outcomes were equidistant. Overall, there is rougher parity of favorable outcomes than we might have expected, given the preponderant military and economic resources of the United States. Of twenty-two total conflicts, the outcomes in eight (thirty-six percent) were closer to the objectives of Mexico, the outcomes in ten (forty-five percent) were closer to the objectives of the United States, and the results in four were equidistant. Given U.S. power over resources, what explains the occasional Mexican power over outcomes? Why did Mexico win any conflicts at all?

Aspects of Conflict Relations: Initiation

Keeping in mind the alternative explanations for conflict outcomes discussed in the Introduction, we shall examine prewar and postwar conflict relations in order to determine which aspects of those relations are associated with outcomes and which are not. One aspect of those relations is conflict initiation. The answer to the question "Who starts an interstate conflict?" depends upon whether starting a conflict is understood as taking an action that disturbs another state, or as a request in response to such an action. In the years before World War II, Mexico took offending actions when it sought to implement provisions of its 1917 Constitution, and the United States made demands in response to those actions when it sought to defend the interests of its aggrieved property owners. Of seven prewar conflicts, Mexico took the offending action in six, while it made the demand in only one. After the war, the pattern was quite different: of fifteen conflicts, Mexico took the offending action in only four, while it made the demand in eleven. This latter pattern is in keeping with our agrument that in the postwar period issues are placed on the agenda, or introduced as bilateral problems, mostly by Mexico, which uses the summit meetings to bring those issues to the attention of the U.S. president. The pattern of conflict initiation, whether measured by offending action or by demand, does not explain outcomes: it reveals who is trying to influence whom, but it is not an explanation for the success or failure of those efforts. In neither the prewar nor the postwar periods is there a clear relationship between who starts a conflict and whom the outcome favors.

Aspects of Conflict Relations: Jurisdiction

We say that a government has jurisdiction when it has effective authority over the issue in conflict: e.g., if Mexico asks the U.S. to reduce the saline content of water flowing into Mexico from the United States, we say that the U.S. has jurisdiction in the conflict. In the prewar years, the Mexicans were defending their domestic policies from efforts by the U.S. to have those policies changed; after the war, the Mexicans were attempting to change U.S. policies. In the earlier period, Mexico had jurisdiction over the resolution of five out of seven conflicts; in the postwar years, it had sole jurisdiction in only one out of fifteen. We might expect governments to win those conflicts in which they have jurisdiction, because it ought to be easier to say no than to force someone else to say yes. And yet, jurisdiction is not closely related to outcomes: both governments occasionally win conflicts in the jurisdiction of the other.

Aspects of Conflict Relations: Transnational Actors

Here we consider only those conflicts in which transnational actors played significant and independent roles in the political process through which the conflicts were resolved. The actors that most frequently played such a role were multinational corporations and owners of foreign land or bonds. An examination of the role of multinational enterprises and of transnational investors in U.S.-Mexican high-level conflicts shows a considerable difference between the prewar and postwar periods. Before World War II, U.S.-based multinational enterprises were involved more intensively and extensively in conflicts between the United States and Mexico than they were after the war. The most important conflicts prior to 1940 arose because Americans doing business in Mexico appealed to the U.S. government for support against the adverse effects of Mexican government action. After the war, multinational enterprises played little role in the most important U.S.-Mexican conflicts. The absence of postwar presidential-level conflicts involving transnational actors cannot be attributed to any massive change in the quantity of American economic stakes in Mexico: by some measures, those stakes have been growing. Rather, U.S.-based multinational corporations have been less involved in U.S.-Mexican postwar conflicts for several other reasons.

One reason is that postwar Mexican governments have been less inclined to seriously threaten these corporations. Although today the state and major foreign investors often disagree vigorously over what the proper role of private foreign investment in Mexico should be, the Mexican government since the 1930s has not drastically changed the rules of the game under which most of those investors operate. Of course, Mexican attitudes toward foreign investment are far from monolithic, and the state has had to assure native entrepreneurs an adequate share of the benefits from economic growth.[27] However, neither official Mexican statements that resurrect the nationalist sentiments of the past nor occasional proposals that worry some businessmen have seriously troubled either foreign investors or bilateral relations. As one historian observed, the "Mexican entrepreneurs shape their strategy in order not to scare (Americans)— to annoy them, which is fair enough, but not to scare them."[28] By and large, postwar Mexican development policies have treated foreign investors well.

Another reason that U.S.-based multinational enterprises have been less important as political actors in postwar conflicts may be that most of the postwar American investment in Mexico has been in manufacturing, rather than in resource extraction. Not only was investment in manufacturing explicitly favored by Mexican government policy, but foreign investment in manufacturing has only recently become a source of friction between investors and developing country host governments. Most of the investor-related conflicts that plagued U.S.-Mexican relations before World War II involved resource extraction, as do many of those that trouble U.S. postwar relations with other countries. That fewer U.S.-based resource exploiters were operating in Mexico after the war than before it, that their economic importance in Mexico was steadily reduced, and that many of the problems between the state and foreign investors were worked out in Mexico before World War II, helps to explain the absence of investor-stimulated conflicts between the two governments. Moreover, in the years after the war, the Mexican government has moved sensitively when political or economic considerations led it to ease foreign firms out of key sectors of the economy, as the history of the Mexican government's takeover of the electrical industry reveals.[29]

A third reason that multinational enterprises have been less involved in postwar conflicts between Mexico and the United States may be that many American businessmen have learned to live with increasing host government control, and that some have even found advantage in it. At least one U.S. investor claimed to welcome increased Mexican government involvement in the economy: "Once we have a deal," he said, "it is easier to get money, easier to get import permits, easier to get appointments, easier to get roads, electricity, sites in industrial plants—easier to do almost anything."[30]

A final reason for the absence of postwar disputes involving U.S.-based firms may be that American firms which have been disturbed by Mexican government actions may have refrained from presenting their case to the U.S. government because of their belief that the government had become less vigorous in support of American businessmen abroad than it once was, and that their appeal for assistance would not be favorably received.

In sum, both the U.S. and Mexican governments as well as foreign investors, have approached post war investor-related disagreements in a manner less calculated to result in high-level interstate friction than was true in the decades before World War II. As a result, multinational enterprises have not been significant political actors in postwar U.S.-Mexican conflicts.

The change in the importance of transnational actors to bilateral conflicts is not matched by a change in their influence over outcomes. In neither the prewar nor the postwar period did the presence of transnational actors determine the outcome of the interstate conflicts. Even in the prewar period, when multinational enterprises were actively involved in conflict negotiations, they often were not able to secure outcomes favorable to their objectives. In several of the prewar conflicts, in fact, a split developed between the U.S. government and the transnational actors whom the government had been supporting. The involvement of transnational actors in U.S.-Mexican conflicts does not help to predict the results of those conflicts.

Aspects of Conflict Relations: Government Cohesion

Students of American foreign policy now inquire as a matter of course into bureaucratic struggles and differences of opinion within the U.S. government in order to understand U.S. policy behavior. Limited evidence suggests that the bureaucratic politics approach is not the most fruitful way to analyze the foreign policy behavior of the Mexican government.

The policy-making process in a country is a reflection of the country's political system, which in postwar Mexico has become consolidated as an authoritarian regime in which the most important source of official power is the president. According to one student of Mexican affairs, the president is "the central figure in the formulation and execution of Mexican foreign policy," by virtue of constitutionally conferred power, "by tradition and expectation of the Mexicans, and by his leadership of the Revolutionary elite and the political apparatus of the nation."[31] In Mexico, where the public, including organized sectors of the official party, is reactive, the judiciary generally passive, and the congress subservient, the president has considerable discretion to set and implement the nation's foreign policies. He is constrained by the elite's policy preferences and by Mexican dependence on the United States, and his flexibility is probably least in the area of foreign economic policy, in which foreign and domestic concerns merge and which impinges directly on the interests of powerful groups. Undoubtedly, however, he sets his country's foreign policy to a much greater extent than the president of the United States sets American foreign policy. In the case of the Mexican political system, it may be misleading to place much emphasis on internal, bureaucratic division, although more empirical evidence on this point is needed.

Because the U.S. foreign policy-making process is more fragmented than that of Mexico, the Mexican government may have taken advantage of, or merely been favored by, bureaucratic divisions and competing policy preferences within the U.S. government. The data indicate, however, that whether the U.S. government was seriously divided or not makes no consistent difference to the outcomes, either before or after World War II. On occasion, though, U.S. divisions did contribute to outcomes preferred by Mexico, as is illustrated by the history of the oil expropriation conflict (1938-1942), which will be discussed below.

Transgovernmental coalitions, in which both governments were divided but in which agencies within each of them allied with each other to work for a common purpose, do not appear in the U.S.-Mexican relationship during the years from 1920 to 1975. This finding is, however, tentative because we know relatively little about the making of Mexican foreign policy. Situations in which the Mexican government, conceived as a whole, worked closely with an agency of the U.S. government to achieve an outcome which both the Mexican government and the particular U.S. agency preferred, appear first during the years after World War II, perhaps because of the rapidly increasing bureaucratic complexity of the U.S. foreign policy-making apparatus.

When division mattered at all to outcomes, it worked to the advantage of the more cohesive Mexican government. For example, during negotiations for a water treaty in the 1940s, Mexican diplomats worked with State Department officials and with Colorado River upper basin state representatives, at the initiative of the State Department, to off-set the opposition to the treaty by California interests and their congressional supporters.[32] And, in the 1960s, the Mexican government joined forces with agribusiness interests and the U.S. Department of Agriculture to argue against the U.S. Department of Labor's opposition to an extension of the bracero treaty.[33] However, the fragmentation of the U.S. decision-making process did not always work to Mexico's advantage. For example, in the 1940s, anxious to secure U.S. congressional support for an oil development loan from a reluctant U.S. executive branch, the Mexican government invited the House Committee on Interstate and Foreign Commerce to tour the Mexican oil fields and to meet with President Miguel Alemán (1946-1952). But Mexican efforts to use the U.S. Congress as an ally against the State Department failed; despite the congressional visit to Mexico, the Mexican government did not get the oil loan it requested.[34]

Aspects of Conflict Relations: Bargaining Tactics

Two prominent bargaining tactics in conflict relations are retaliation and linkage. Retaliation differs from linkage in that the first occurs within a particular conflict (e.g., if you restrict my trade, I'll restrict yours), while the second joins conflicts (if you join an oil cartel, I'll restrict your trade).

Neither before nor after World War II does retaliation appear to have been a common bargaining tactic on the part of either government, although when it was used it worked. For example, during the long course of the water division controversy, each government used irrigation works and dam projects to pressure the opposing side in a conflict that ended in compromise. In the 1930s the U.S. was forced to negotiate on Colorado River usage because of Mexican projects that threatened to affect the flow of lower Rio Grande water; when the U.S. in turn decided upon an irrigation project on its side of the Rio Grande, Mexico became more flexible in negotiations over usage of the two rivers.[35] For another example, after World War II, retaliation by the U.S. secured for it a favorable outcome in the 1950s bracero program conflict. The U.S. government, angered by Mexico's unwillingness to respond favorably to U.S. requests for a renegotiation of various aspects of the program, broke off talks and initiated a unilateral program of Mexican worker recruitment. On the day the U.S. program began, thousands of Mexican workers ignored their government's orders to stay away from the border and rushed to the U.S. side en masse; the Mexican government shortly thereafter accepted most of the American requests for renegotiation.[36] In 1969, to note a last example, the U.S., frustrated in its efforts to secure greater Mexican cooperation in fighting the drug traffic, retaliated by initiating a program of intensive search at border crossing points. Soon after the search program (known as Operation Intercept) began, the Mexican government agreed to extend greater cooperation. In sum, although retaliation was used infrequently, it was used more often by the United States against Mexico, and it appears to have worked when used.

In contrast, linkage is not consistently related to outcomes. In the decades before World War II, each government used linkage as a bargaining tactic against the other. In the early 1920s, for example, the Harding administration tied a Mexican request for recognition of the new government in that country after the overthrow of the old one to a U.S. demand for a treaty of "amity and commerce" which would embody guarantees to American owners of property in Mexico.[37] Although the Obregón government wanted U.S. recognition badly, it declined the deal, believing that it infringed on national dignity and that the political costs of seeming to surrender to American blackmail would be too high. When the Mexican government agreed to hold informal talks at which the outstanding disputes between the two governments would be discussed, the U.S. government, faced with the failure of the coercive approach, retreated from its insistence on a prior treaty. In exchange for informal agreements on several issues reached in the talks, the U.S. government granted recognition to the government of Álvaro Obregón. The U.S. linkage of protection for American property owners in Mexico and recognition of the Mexican government brought Mexico to the table for placating talks, but it did not secure for the United States the desired treaty or any binding international agreements.

Just as refusal to grant recognition was a linkage tactic used by the United States, so may involvement in Nicaragua have been one used by Mexico. In the mid-1920s, the United States protested Mexican policies pertaining to agrarian reform and to ownership of petroleum resources. At the same time, the U.S. was becoming increasingly involved in a struggle in Nicaragua, where the Liberals were attempting to depose the U.S.-backed Conservative president. In 1926, the Mexican government responded favorably to a request for aid from Nicaraguan Liberals by providing material support, an action which was related to Mexican tensions with the United States and which led President Calvin Coolidge to demand before the U.S. Congress that Mexico stop its intervention in Nicaragua.[38] In 1927, when the governments of Mexico and the United States began to seek an improvement in their relations for reasons quite apart from Nicaragua, Mexico ceased its aid to the Liberals and the Nicaraguan issue disappeared from the U.S.-Mexican conflict agenda.

In the decades after World War II, different issues usually were not linked. However, during the oil loan conflict in the early postwar years, the U.S. used a *quid pro quo* to try and change Mexican policy. Throughout the 1940s the U.S. attempted to pressure Mexico into permitting private foreign oil firms to participate in the development of the Mexican petroleum industry by holding as hostage a loan for petroleum development which the Mexican government had requested from the Export-Import Bank. Mexico eventually received a much smaller loan than the amount it originally requested, and it was granted a loan only because President Harry Truman believed the loan necessary in order to preserve economic stability in Mexico. The *quid pro quo* did not work for the United States: Mexico steadfastly refused to permit the reentry of private foreign oil firms.[39]

The only conflict in which linkage appears to have influenced the outcome was the oil expropriation conflict of 1938-1942, which will be discussed below. Over all, linkage tactics were occasionally used but infrequently successful in U.S.-Mexican conflict relations.

Aspects of Conflict Relations: Bargaining Position

The bargaining position of each government's executive is determined in part by the intensity with which each government can pursue its objectives vis-à-vis the other. In the U.S.-Mexican case the prewar and postwar decades differed considerably in terms of the relative level of each government's concern with the relationship and, consequently, in terms of the relative attention and intensity which each government could bring to the conflict negotiations.

Before the war, when most of the conflicts raised emotions and commanded considerable presidential and public attention on both sides of the border, there was greater symmetry of concern; after the war, the U.S. president and bureaucracy turned most of their attention elsewhere, while growing Mexican sensitivity to dependence on the United States assured that Mexican concern with U.S. policies would remain high.

We might expect that greater attention and concern with the outcomes of the conflicts would have been an advantage for the Mexicans, that the fragmentation of U.S. global concerns would have meant that the U.S. lost conflicts to Mexico because it could not muster the attention to pursue its short-run interests effectively. However, if fragmentation of U.S. attention were the explanation for Mexican successes in postwar conflicts, we would wonder why the U.S. has won its fair share of those conflicts.

More important than the fragmentation of U.S. attention and concern is the process of politicization in the United States, which determined the political costs to the U.S. president of assent to Mexican requests and the flexibility with which he could respond to those requests. When the political costs of assent to the Mexican requests were low, or when the U.S. executive had relative flexibility in negotiations, as was true in the conflicts over "El Chamizal" and over the salinity of Colorado River water, the outcomes consistently favored Mexico. In contrast, when the political costs were high, or serious external and internal constraints on the U.S. president's negotiating flexibility existed, as was true in trade conflicts, the results consistently favored the United States.

Explaining Outcomes

The low political costs of some outcomes may explain why the U.S. president was able to accede to occasional Mexican postwar requests, but it does not explain why he agreed to do so. The major source of postwar Mexican power over outcomes was the implicit link between assent to Mexican requests and the continuation of stability within Mexico and in the bilateral relationship. After World War II, the U.S. was concerned to protect its strategic and economic interests in Latin America, which it considered to be within its sphere of influence. As the hegemonic power in the region, the U.S. had the resources and the will to set limits to permissible behavior by other, formally sovereign states.[40] Although on occasion the U.S. used its military and economic might to insure that the foreign and domestic policies of Latin American states did not diverge too far from U.S. policy preferences, it did not have to make its ability to enforce its preferences explicit for Mexico. Internal and external constraints operating on Mexican policy makers assured that U.S. interests would not be seriously threatened and that the U.S. would not be forced to exercise overtly its military and economic power.

Mexico was willing to seek to manage conflict in order to preserve the gains it received from its close ties to the United States. Some of those gains were non-governmental and transnational in nature (e.g., tourist and investment dollars), but others rested upon occasionally favorable U.S. responses to Mexican requests (e.g., decreasing the saline content of Colorado River water entering Mexico). Throughout the postwar period the United States has on occasion been willing to pay in unfavorable outcomes (in what are, from its perspective, relatively unimportant conflicts) the cost of maintaining a system that is to its overall advantage.

This advantageous system explains why the U.S. assented to occasional Mexican requests. The explanation of why it did not assent to Mexican requests in other conflicts must take into account both the fragmented nature of decision-making in the U.S. and the process through which some conflicts are politicized. In effect, bureaucratic agencies and non-governmental influences are at work in the U.S. political system; they often compete with the pressures to satisfy Mexican requests, and sometimes have the political clout to secure their wishes. The process of politicization explains why Mexico has consistently lost in the conflicts over the issues most important in both countries: trade.

Trade conflicts are a form of economic conflict which involves commercial relations between countries. The outcomes in the conflicts in which trade was the issue run counter to the overall pattern of outcomes, in which Mexico does well in achieving its objectives. Before World War II, trade relations did not cause high-level conflicts between the United States and Mexico. In contrast, after the war trade accounts for some 37 percent of all conflicts, and of the six trade disputes, the outcomes in five favored the United States. In the postwar period, among all kinds of issues, Mexico has done worst in trade conflicts, and the United States has done best.

Trade policy is both domestic and foreign policy. The U.S. executive sometimes can offset the organized domestic interests that push for restrictive trade policies by countering with arguments of more important national considerations. Particular private sector interests in the U.S., however, have had an inordinate influence on the making of U.S. policy toward Latin America, including Mexico. Even when the State Department has supported a Mexican trade request, the ability of the department to have its recommendation accepted as executive branch policy has often been slight. More often, the Bureau of Inter-American Affairs has had trouble having its position accepted within the State Department. In addition, the trade area is one in which other executive branch departments and the Congress are quick to promote their own interests and to respond to their own constituencies. Furthermore, labor has been a potent political force and its calls for protection have been difficult for any administration to ignore. The Mexicans therefore have had difficulty getting favorable outcomes in trade disputes because the stakes for politically powerful and organized groups are high. This has made accession to Mexican requests costly for U.S. presidents or even impossible because of legislative constraints on presidential freedom of action.

In addition, trade problems are often treated as global rather than as regional issues by U.S. government agencies which are not specifically concerned with U.S. relations with Mexico. Most U.S. trade conflicts with Mexico also affect other developing nations, in Latin America or elsewhere, so the issues in dispute can be particularized for Mexico in only one way: by U.S. acknowledgement that a common border entitles Mexico to special consideration. This situation is well recognized by Mexico; in 1969, the Mexican Minister of Industry and Commerce told a special commission headed by Nelson Rockefeller that the U.S. should accept Mexico's "right on all economic levels to be given border nation treatment."[41] Much rhetoric about the special historic and geographic ties that bind the two neighboring countries passes over the border in both directions (perhaps the only aspect of the transnational exchange that is coequal), but Mexico has not been able to gain individualized treatment on what the U.S. sees as multilateral issues. That Mexico has not been able or willing to do much about its consistent inability to secure some of its especially desired trade concessions from the United States is the clearest evidence of the severly limited nature of Mexican power over outcomes.

The Oil Expropriation Conflict

It is possible that the search for patterns may disguise the reality of individual cases. This section attempts to show what led to the outcome in one dispute—the conflict over oil expropriation (1938-1942).

The most salient U.S.-Mexican conflict of the 20th century was brought to a head in March 1938, when the Mexican government expropriated the properties of major foreign oil corporations.[42] The labor dispute that eventually led to the expropriation occurred at a time (1936) when U.S.-Mexican relations were already troubled by an agrarian reform program in Mexico and by controversies over debts and claims. Some U.S. officials, including Secretary of State Cordell Hull and Under Secretary Sumner Welles, were not pleased by developments in Mexico and were prepared to listen sympathetically to the oilmens' complaints.

Their representations on behalf of the oil firms, however, did not deter the Mexican government from insisting that the companies adhere to executive and judicial decisions that they increase wage and supplementary benefits for oil workers. When the companies refused to obey the law, their properties were expropriated.

For the next several years, the petroleum issue dominated U.S.-Mexican relations. The companies appealed to the U.S. government for support and sought nothing less than the return of the properties or compensation, including payment for oil still in the ground. The U.S. demanded arbitration and argued that Mexico must pay prompt, adequate, and effective compensation for expropriated properties. The Mexican government would not consider reentry of the oil firms, admitted the obligation to pay some compensation, refused to do so for subsoil oil, and rejected the arbitration demand. For each side, the stakes were high: the Americans were anxious to preserve what they considered the Western rule of international law and property rights, the Mexicans saw their national sovereignty threatened. In the end, the U.S. supported an outcome that was closer to the objectives of Mexico. Why was Mexico able to secure an outcome that favored its objectives in a major conflict with the United States?

From March 1938 through the spring of 1940, the U.S. government tried several tactics to effect a change in Mexican policy, but without success. When the Mexican government rejected the U.S. demand for arbitration, the U.S. seriously began to consider a Mexican proposal for appointment of a bilateral commission to determine the amount of compensation. The U.S. government spent most of the next year vainly trying to gain oil company support for the commission proposal; but gradually it moved away from the company position toward that of the Mexican government. The reason seems to have been the growing threat of war, and the desire of U.S. officials to secure Mexican cooperation in hemisphere defense plans. In a conversation with American officials in June 1940, the Mexican ambassador explained that Mexico was prepared to cooperate, but that "The necessary basis for joint military action in an emergency is a general political agreement between the two countries."[43] In the spring of 1941, with the War Department's increasing eagerness for the use of air bases in Mexico, the need for a settlement became critical. In November 1941, the U.S. and Mexico signed a comprehensive agreement in which several prewar bilateral conflicts were resolved; the agreement included preliminary resolution of the oil expropriation conflict and acceptance of the idea of establishing a bilateral commission to determine the amount of compensation for the expropriated properties.

One Mexican official at the time stated that the U.S. had the military and economic resources to force a favorable policy change by Mexico, but that it chose not to use those resources. This is true, of course, for every conflict between the U.S. and Mexico, both before and after World War II. We want to know why the U.S. chose not to use its superior resources to force Mexico to change its policy. A realist interpretation would attribute U.S. restraint to the dominance of the national security threat, which created a compelling need for Mexican cooperation. The military-security issue is seen to take precedence over the economic conflict and the definition of the national interest is supposed to change as the international circumstances require. Thus, a world power makes a concession to a weaker nation in exchange for that country's cooperation in a more important matter. The weaker state gains a favorable conflict outcome because the stronger state makes a trade-off. At first glance, the military-security link appears to have determined the outcome of the conflict, conforming neatly to a realist understanding of international affairs.

We cannot know for certain how the Roosevelt administration would have dealt with Mexico had U.S. officials not been worried about fascism in the hemisphere, but we can speculate on the basis of what we do know. We know, for instance, that Mexico had rejected U.S. arbitration demands and that it was prepared to suffer the consequences of the application of greater economic pressure by the United States. We know also that the U.S. was unwilling to use greater pressure than that already applied for reasons quite apart from the defense-related concern. Those reasons are worth considering.

First, within the Roosevelt administration there was considerable sympathy for the social and economic reforms introduced in Mexico by the administration of Lázaro Cárdenas (1934-1940). To many Americans in and out of government, changing private and public sector relations in Mexico were reminiscent of the New Deal in the U.S., a view expressed on several occasions by Franklin Roosevelt himself. Second, the U.S. administration was concerned with the Good Neighbor Policy and with overall U.S. relations with the Americas. Its actions in the oil expropriation conflict were thus constrained by the prior enunciation of a policy that became the standard by which the U.S. would be judged throughout Latin America. While dealing with Mexico, the U.S. president was reminded by U.S. and Latin American officials that the Good Neighbor Policy was receiving its critical test and that its fate might well depend upon U.S. handling of the oil controversy. Third, strong domestic countervailing pressures existed in the United States. When the U.S. government tried to use a silver purchase agreement as an instrument of pressure against Mexico in the oil case, it quickly discovered that the major losers would be American mining firms, which opposed the application of economic sanctions.

When the Mexicans rejected the U.S. demand for arbitration, the U.S. was left with three alternatives: escalate the pressure in an effort to effect a change in Mexican policy; let the expropriation issue drag on, clouding bilateral relations; or adopt the Mexican proposal for a settlement. Reasons apart from the military concern kept the U.S. from escalating the pressure, and it is difficult to imagine that so serious an issue would have been allowed to fester. The only feasible alternative was to accept the Mexican proposal. The military-security concern associated with the onset of World War II, in this view, affected the timing more than the substance of the settlement; eventually, Mexico and the U.S. would have come to a similar agreement. If the U.S. concern with military security did not by itself explain the outcome of this conflict, what else mattered?

When we leave the level of general security interests and look at the bargaining positions, we find some aspects that worked to Mexico's advantage. For one thing, the United States was seeking to change Mexican policy. All Mexico had to do was refuse: refuse to give the property back, refuse to arbitrate, refuse to pay. A second aspect of the bargaining process was that the Mexicans were not without recourse against U.S. economic sanctions. Faced with a worldwide boycott of Mexican oil imposed by the major multinational oil firms, the Mexicans turned to the fascist governments of Germany and Italy for barter agreements. As the possibility of selling to the fascists lessened the pressure on Mexico, it increased it for the Americans, whose concern over economic defense of the hemisphere was growing. Third, the Mexican government was much more cohesive and unified in support of its position than the U.S. was in support of its stance in the conflict. Cárdenas already had organized the agrarian and labor sectors of the population for internal political purposes, and they backed him during this challenge to national sovereignty. U.S. officials accepted Cárdenas' claim that the Mexican nation would accept the suffering brought about by economic sanctions before it would submit to oil company or U.S. government pressure.[44] As the willingness of the Mexicans to suffer seemed to grow, the leverage required of the U.S. to effect a change in Mexican policy also increased, and, for reasons already discussed, the U.S. was at no point willing to greatly escalate the pressure.

In contrast to the Mexican government, the U.S. government, as already remarked, lacked cohesion and unity in its approach to the oil issue. Hull, Welles, and other State Department officials tended to take an inflexible and legalistic position. U.S. Ambassador Josephus Daniels and Secretary of the Treasury Henry Morgenthau were more sympathetic to reforms in Mexico and more concerned about the possibility of fascist penetration in that country. Roosevelt was thus barraged with conflicting advice, and this conflict within the administration lessened the ability of the U.S. government to pursue any position vigorously.

The explanation for the outcome of the oil expropriation conflict is complex. Bargaining position mattered: the Mexican government was backed by a mobilized and supportive population in a conflict over which it had jurisdiction and about which it was unified. The stakes in cooperation also mattered: the growing menace of fascism contributed to division within the U.S. government and stimulated the U.S. to seek a settlement more quickly than it might have if no such threat had existed. For reasons of both structure of interests and bargaining position, the U.S. government in the end was willing to change its definition of what an acceptable outcome would be. In refusing to assent to American demands until that change came about lay the true Mexican power over the outcome.

4. The Canadian Comparison

The question of how the national characteristics of Mexico and Canada shape the relations of those countries with the United States deserves more extensive study than we can give it here, but we can at least suggest some of the differences in their conflict relations with the United States, and in the process hint at some of the ways that politics among the industrialized nations differs from politics between the developing nations and the industrialized world.

The relationships of both Mexico and Canada with the U.S. abound in similarities: a common border with the United States, the increase of transnational flows and intergovernmental contacts, the inequality of the military and economic relationships, penetration by U.S.-based multinational corporations, the minimal role of force, and domination of the conflict agendas by socio-economic issues. Moreover, both nations are dependent on the United States, with whom they share similar terms of trade and investment.[45] The U.S. takes most of each nation's exports, provides most of its imports, and supplies the greater part of its foreign investment. The conditions of both bilateral relationships appear to approximate those of complex interdependence. Yet differences in the bilateral relationships are more important than the similarities. Both Mexico and Canada are dependent countries, but Canada has a much larger gross national product and a much smaller population, growing at a much slower rate, than Mexico. Furthermore, its political system, cultural heritage, and major language are, in contrast to Mexico's almost identical with those of the United States. Thus, although both nations border the U.S., the decades old judgement of an American scholar of Mexican affairs that "in its spirit, outlook, and heritage, Mexico remains a faraway land" still stands.[46] Mexico is Latin American, developing, and authoritarian; Canada is Anglo-French, industrialized, and democratic. And, although heavy and multiple transnational flows connect both Mexico and Canada to the United States, the inequality in the direction of flows and in the sensitivity to dependence on them is much greater in the Mexican case. For its part, the U.S. is far more sensitive to the behavior of the Canadian government than it is to that of Mexican administrations. Finally, Mexico generally has not sought to play Canada's middle power role in world affairs.

How are the differences reflected in conflict relations with the United States? For one thing, the U.S.-Canadian conflict agenda was larger, and changed more over time, than the Mexican one.[47] Before World War II, as Table 3 shows, the U.S. presidential agenda contained one more Canadian than Mexican conflict; after the war, it had sixteen more conflicts with Canada than with Mexico. Clearly, the U.S. president devoted more time after World War II to Canada than he did to Mexico. Not only were the U.S. and Canada engaged in conflict more frequently in the postwar period than the U.S. and Mexico, but they opposed each other over a greater variety of issues (see Table 3). The complexity of the U.S.-Canadian postwar agenda reflects the military and political importance of Canada in the postwar world. The U.S. and Canada opposed each other at the highest level over a variety of problems, as might be expected of two developed nations, while most U.S.-Mexican postwar conflicts involved trade or migrants.

Differences in the pattern of conflict initiation were greater in the postwar than in the prewar decades. In the prewar period, as Table 4 shows, most conflicts between the U.S. and both Canada and Mexico arose from U.S. government requests. During the postwar decades conflict initiation between the U.S. and Canada was more balanced. In the U.S.-Mexican relationship, Mexico now initiated most requests.

In terms of the overall pattern of outcomes in conflicts with the United States, Mexico and Canada are relatively well-balanced (see Table 5), but there is considerable change over time. The U.S. did better in its postwar conflicts with Mexico than it had in its prewar conflicts, while it

COMPARISON TABLES

TABLE 3: CONFLICTS BY ISSUE AREA

	Military Security	Diplo-matic	Eco-nomic	Joint Resource	Competing Sovereignty	Total
Prewar						
U.S.-Mexico	0	2	4	1	0	7
U.S.-Canada	0	0	5	3	0	8
Postwar						
U.S.-Mexico	0	0	12	2	1	15
U.S.-Canada	7	6	11	3	4	31

TABLE 4: CONFLICT INITIATION

Conflict placed on agenda by

	United States	Canada or Mexico
Prewar		
U.S.-Mexico	6	1
U.S.-Canada	5	3
Postwar		
U.S.-Mexico	4	11
U.S. -Canada	12	19

TABLE 5: CONFLICT BY OUTCOMES

Outcome closer to the objectives of

	Mexico	U.S.	Equi-distant	Total	Canada	U.S.	Equi-distant	Total
Prewar	3	2	2	7	2	5	1	8
Postwar	5	8	2	15	14	11	6	31
Total	8	10	4	22	16	16	7	39

TABLE 6: POSTWAR OUTCOMES BY CONFLICT ISSUE AREA

Outcome closer to the objectives of

Issue Area	Mexico	U.S.	Equi-distant	Canada	U.S.	Equi-distant
Military Security	0	0	0	2	4	1
Diplomatic	0	0	0	4	2	0
Trade*	1	5	0	4	2	0
Other Socio-economic	2	2	2	1	1	3
Joint Resource	1	1	0	1	0	2
Competing Sovereignty	1	0	0	2	2	0

*For purposes of this table and the related discussion, trade is considered a separate issue area, distinguished from other economic issues by its involvement of commercial relations.

did much worse in its postwar conflicts with Canada than it had done before the war. In terms of specific issue areas, the only striking contrast in postwar outcomes in an area in which both Mexico and Canada conflicted with the U.S. is trade, where Canada's postwar record is best and Mexico's is worst (see Table 6). The numbers are small but revealing. Canada secured outcomes favorable to its objectives in four out of six postwar trade conflicts.[48] In contrast, Mexico secured an outcome favorable to it in only one out of six, and the one success occurred in the 1940s. Why does Canada do better than Mexico in trade conflicts with the United States?

For one thing, Canadian-U.S. trade relations can be more easily isolated from trade relations with other nations in the hemisphere. The U.S. can more easily assent to Canadian requests without adjusting its trade policy throughout all of Latin America. Also, between the U.S. and Canada there has been a common, mutually preferential trade regime, which has not been true of the lopsided exchanges between the U.S. and Mexico. On trade issues, Mexico has had little to offer the United States.

It is tempting to attribute Canadian success in trade conflicts to the influence of transnational actors, which have been far more involved in postwar U.S.-Canadian conflicts than in U.S.-Mexican disputes. In some conflicts, transnational actors did help the Canadian government to secure preferred results, but in trade disputes their effect appears divided: of six U.S.-Canadian trade conflicts in which transnational actors were involved, each side won three.

Several reasons may explain the greater importance of transnational actors to postwar U.S.-Canadian than to U.S.-Mexican conflicts. For one thing, transnational actors have not been involved in U.S.-Mexican postwar conflicts for reasons which have already been discussed. For another, because the U.S. government has requested relatively little of postwar Mexican administrations, it has had no incentive to use transnational actors to help secure policy changes in Mexico in the same way in which it has tried to use such actors in its relations with Canada. In the postwar period, the pattern of requests runs from Mexico to the United States. Third, Mexico has not tried to use transnational actors to secure concessions from the U.S. as Canada has used such actors, because the issues in conflict have not concerned those actors directly, and possibly because Mexico has been unwilling to jeopardize through the use of such actors the goods, capital, and technology that it receives from the United States. Finally, the greater use of such actors by the government of Canada is due to language similarity, familiarity with the political system of the United States, and greater diplomatic skill.

Intergovernmental alliances also have helped the Canadians more than the Mexicans, although this is a source of power over outcomes for Canada which has not proved important in trade conflicts. Of the eight U.S.-Canadian conflicts in which such coalitions were important, the Canadians secured their objectives in five, only one of which was a trade dispute. Still, Mexico cannot claim intergovernmental coalitions as a source of power in any trade conflict. The greater concentration of decision-making authority in Mexico as compared to Canada and the more traditional approach of Mexican diplomats may explain the smaller role of intergovernmental coalitions in the U.S.-Mexican relationship.

The brief comparison of U.S. conflict relations with Canada and Mexico reveals that both Canada and Mexico do better in terms of securing preferred outcomes in conflicts with the United States than we might have expected, given the greater resources of the United States. However, the Canadians enjoy greater gains from their relationship with the U.S. than do the Mexicans, at least as measured by satisfactory results in trade disputes, which are of most importance to both Canada and Mexico. This Canadian power over outcomes derived from the close approximation of U.S.-Canadian relations to the conditions of complex interdependence, conditions which assured that the U.S. and Canada were much more evenly balanced in their sensitivity and importance to each other than were the U.S. and Mexico. Mexican power over outcomes depended upon low political costs for the U.S. president and was limited to the relative ease of U.S. assent to occasional Mexican requests, to preserve behavior within Mexico and between Mexico and the U.S. that U.S. officials deemed important.

5. Whither Dependence?

In the 1970s economic instability brought new forms of bargaining between rich and poor countries. Mexico, of course, participated in these developments. In 1970, Luis Echeverría succeeded Gustavo Díaz Ordaz (1964-1970) as President of Mexico, after having served as Minister of Interior in a regime perhaps best known for the government massacre of several hundred protesting students in Mexico City on the eve of the 1968 summer Olympic games. A popular interpretation of Mexican politics holds that presidential policies exhibit a pendulum-like swing from left of center to right of center, as each administration corrects the excessive tendencies of its predecessor.[49] Because the regime of Díaz Ordaz catered too much to the right, by this interpretation Echeverría had to adjust by redressing some of the grievances of the left, and the Mexican left had long urged a more independent stance vis-à-vis the U.S. in Mexican foreign policies.

In any case, after 1971, the foreign policy of the Echeverría administration seemed to become less accommodating to American sensitivities.[50] The Mexican government actively supported the Allende regime in Chile and broke relations with the military junta that overthrew it, and, as already noted, it voted in favor of the U.N. resolution equating Zionism with racism. Another aspect of the regime's foreign policy was an ostensible move away from concentration on the special relationship with the U.S. and toward the stimulation of Latin American unity.[51] Mexico was visibly in the forefront of efforts to form political and economic alliances within the hemisphere and beyond, for the purpose of promoting Latin American development and of achieving bargaining advantages vis-à-vis the United States and other industrialized nations. During most of the postwar years the U.S. and Mexico had refrained from bringing their bilateral problems to multilateral forums, but the inability of the Mexican government to gain special consideration when the U.S. levied an import surcharge on manufactured imports in August 1971 led Echeverría's advisers to take a dim view of exclusive reliance on bilateral discussions. Meanwhile, the peripatetic president, accompanied by a corps of economists and technical advisers, traveled to and hosted meetings with leaders from many countries. At home, Echeverría sponsored legislation which, the president claimed, would obtain for the Mexican people greater benefits from the import of foreign technology, encourage foreign investors to locate their operations in the poorer regions of the country away from the crowded Mexican metropolitan areas, and direct the new foreign investment into export sectors of the Mexican economy.

All these maneuvers gave the impression of considerable challenge to the structures of dependence binding Mexico to the United States, an impression that was reinforced by Echeverría's aggressive rhetoric. It is not likely, however, that his actions were intended as a serious challenge to Mexican ties with the United States; rather, they helped the official party domestically and also served as a stepping stone for the president, who hoped to move from his country's highest office into a position of international prestige based upon his activities on behalf of the developing nations.

Whatever the purposes of the administration's behavior, Echeverría ran afoul of structural economic realities and of private sector suspicions. The combination of heavy government spending, increases in public services and wages, and substantial foreign borrowing, all in a period of international recession, predictably produced rapid and sustained inflation in Mexico. Meanwhile, the wave of terrorism that plagued many countries hit Mexico's largest cities. As inflation, rhetoric, and public tension mounted, the Mexican private sector responded by attributing most of the country's ills to the Echeverría regime, by refusing to invest, and by exporting capital.

Several weeks before leaving office, and in the midst of severe economic difficulties, the administration announced the end of the peso's 22-year old parity with the dollar. The peso, the government declared, would be allowed to float: abruptly, the exchange rate dropped from 12.5 to about 22.5 pesos to the dollar. Moreover, it appeared that Mexico was not ready for this long overdue economic move. Inflation continued, unemployment remained high, and the value of the peso fluctuated wildly, creating panic in the financial community and increasing loss of confidence in the government. As though to add fuel to the fire, Echeverría declared just before leaving office that numerous private landholdings in the wheat-rich state of Sonora were illegal, an act which stimulated increased tension in the countryside and which generated long unheard rumors of a coup. By the end of his administration, Echeverría's domestic and foreign policies had generated considerable uncertainty among important segments of the private sectors in Mexico and the United States and had aroused the concern of watchful U.S. officials. Clearly, all was not well with Mexico.

Throughout the last months of the Echeverría administration, President-elect José López Portillo managed to give the impression of remaining aloof from and uninvolved with these troublesome events. With the placating messages and accommodating actions that followed his inaguration in December 1976, much of the public furor subsided.

Still, the private sector in both countries remained suspicious, U.S. officials and tourists were watchful, and the Mexican economy was, obviously, in very bad shape. According to the Banco de México's annual report, real gross domestic product grew only by two percent in 1976, the lowest rise since 1953; moreover, the consumer price rise of twenty-seven percent was the highest since the early 1950s.[52] 1977, it appeared, promised more high inflation and low production.

In order to bring the economy back into reasonable shape, the Mexican government required the cooperation of the private sectors in Mexico and in the United States, as well as of the U.S. government. None of those actors on whose cooperation the Mexican government depended were internally cohesive and they did not share many policy preferences, but all applauded the new administration's moves away from the rhetoric and from some of the behavior of its predecessor. Where Echeverría had criticized and threatened the national private sector, López Portillo cajoled and enticed; now the businessmen were asked to help in an alliance for production and were promised tax advantages and other benefits in exchange for investment in priority areas. Where Echeverría had extensively borrowed abroad, López Portillo accepted an agreement with the International Monetary Fund, under which the public sector external debt would be sharply limited for three years. By early January 1977, *Business Latin America* reported to its corporate readership that the new administration "had demonstrated just the kind of pragmatic management abilities needed to effect a recovery." Nevertheless, "If the recovery does go sour," the newsletter warned, "it would not be a slight or slow development, but a rush toward disaster that would make Mexico an extremely risky place to be doing business."[53]

The United States, as López Portillo took pains to point out in his state visit to Washington in February 1977, stands to lose much more than profits, should Mexico "rush toward disaster." For one thing, economic collapse could lead to increased social turmoil, which could result in a Mexican government much less respectful of democratic forms and human rights than the present regime. Mexico does not now present a human rights problem for the U.S. government, as do Argentina, Brazil, Chile, or Uruguay. Whereas Latin American governments of the 1950s waved the threat of Communism in order to gain attention and extract concessions from the United States, Mexico is now bargaining with the threat of something that may be closer to right-wing authoritarianism. Explicitly, the Mexican president has connected U.S. policy to internal conditions in Mexico, and the conditions in Mexico to overall U.S. foreign policy interests.

The U.S. government has yet another reason to be concerned with the

Mexican economy: two U.S. domestic problems, the supply of illegal drugs and the presence of illegal aliens, derive at least in part from economic conditions in Mexico. When López Porillo observed on his Washington trip that "many of the problems that bother you the most are closely related to our economic problems," he again made explicit the link between conditions in Mexico and U.S. interests.

In terms of political importance, the problem of drugs pales beside that of illegal migration from Mexico to the United States. Since the rule of Porfirio Díaz, large numbers of Mexicans have reacted to economic hardship or social turmoil in their own country and to the expectation of better earnings or opportunities in the United States by trying to cross the border, legally if they might, illegally if they must.[54] Although at times (e.g., during World War II and from 1948-1964) the U.S. and Mexican governments cooperated in the administration of programs through which Mexicans were permitted and encouraged to go to the U.S. as temporary workers ("braceros"), the termination of the bracero program in 1964 and the increasingly troubled economic conditions in Mexico have stimulated an increase in the number of illegal crossings.

Estimates of the number of undocumented Mexicans living in the United States vary considerably, from four million to as many as twelve million.[55] The number of illegal Mexican aliens apprehended by the Immigration and Naturalization Service has increased from about 50,000 in 1965 to over 700,000 in 1975.[56] Most realize that the border crossing is dangerous and expensive, and the prospect of finding a job uncertain even if they escape apprehension.[57] But approximately 30 percent of those caught by the Border Patrol are repeaters, some making the effort ten times.[58] The most migration-prone groups, according to one student of the movement of Mexicans to the United States, are landless agricultural workers and sharecroppers, who enter the U.S. not only because of rural unemployment, but because of the lack of well-paying jobs and the huge wage differential between Mexico and the United States.[59] In perhaps no other way is the difference in levels of development between the advanced industrial nations and the developing world so starkly revealed as in this massive and continuing international migration of labor.

The massive exodus does provide several benefits to Mexico. One, Mexicans who do find work in the United States send substantial portions of their U.S. earnings to their families in villages and towns back home, and most are able to save and to return with additional funds. The total amount returned to Mexico through remittances and savings is probably in excess of 3 billion dollars per year,[60] an amount which not only would favorably affect Mexico's balance of payments, but which must alleviate some distress among the country's rural poor. "At the level of the local community in Mexico the impact of migrants' earnings is difficult to overestimate."[61] Second, the migration has functioned much as a frontier, attracting persons who, in the Mexican economic system, may well have grown restless and politically volatile had there been no chance of moving north in order to improve personal and family incomes.[62]

The issue of illegal Mexicans attracted press and congressional attention in the United States as unemployment rose, as labor unions continued to complain that the aliens were taking jobs from American workers, as local communities protested the heavier welfare burdens that, they asserted, were caused by illegal aliens.[63] As with most other U.S.-Mexican problems, the United States can do nothing directly about illegal Mexican workers that will not have a serious impact on Mexico's economy, and perhaps on social and political stability in that country.[64] Cooperative U.S. action on several fronts is a prerequisite to the most comprehensive solution, one based upon economic recovery in Mexico. No matter which way the Mexican government moves, U.S. reactions are critical. On the one hand, anti-inflationary policies will increase urban industrial unemployment and dissatisfaction in the countryside, increasing as well, at least in the short run, pressure for Mexicans to enter the U.S. to work, legally or illegally; their continued ability to enter the U.S. and for those already there to remain will be very important to the Mexican government. On the other hand, if the Mexican government opts for a more dynamic strategy of export-led growth, as seems to be the case, trade concessions from the United States take on increased importance. This unavoidable need for U.S. cooperation leads Mexico to adopt a more yielding posture with respect to bilateral conflict issues, such as the negotiated release of Americans held in Mexican jails on various drug charges.

Of much more concern to the United States government is Mexico's new potential as an oil exporting country. The revelation of a huge Mexican oil find in the fall of 1974 even led to the rare introduction of explicit linkage tactics in bilateral bargaining. The Echeverría government hinted that Mexico might associate with the Organization of Petroleum Exporting countries (OPEC), while the U.S. government, not to be outdone, reminded Mexico that it faced sanctions under the Trade Act of 1974 if it joined the oil cartel.[65] If this jockeying over Mexico's OPEC membership was a game of bluff, neither side saw an advantage in calling the other: Mexico did not join OPEC and no sanctions were applied. Still, the central questions remained: how much oil would

Mexico produce, at what price, and for whom?

In this regard, the U.S. government had reason to be pleased with the early petroleum policy of the López Portillo administration. Although the Mexican government refused to undercut OPEC price levels,[66] it talked less of seeking customers for its petroleum exports beyond the United States. Mexico's only other customer was Israel, whose share of Mexican oil exports has been relatively small.[67] Moreover, Mexico shipped additional oil and natural gas to the United States during the harsh winter of 1976-1977. Most important, the Mexican government is moving forward quickly on the development of increased production capabilities. Official projections from PEMEX, the state oil agency, are for a doubling of production by 1982 and for a sevenfold increase in oil exports.[68] The precise size of the Mexican oil find is unclear (estimates run as high as 60 billion barrels), but it is likely that Mexico will have enough to help insulate the U.S. from the pressure of Middle Eastern oil producers, should it choose to do so. In the coming decade, then, Mexican oil may well benefit the U.S. no less than Mexico.

Mexican cooperation on prisoner exchanges, access to petroleum, cooling of third world rhetoric, and adoption of orthodox fiscal and monetary policies will please private investors and public officials in the United States, and will help to keep the agenda of diplomatic dispute within bounds. Whether it will produce the U.S. behavior sought by Mexico remains to be seen. Although trade concessions from the U.S. remain a top priority for the Mexican government, there is no similar sense of urgency in Washington. The U.S. disposition toward Mexico will depend, as ever, upon the uncertain outcome of protracted legislative and bureaucratic struggles within the U.S. political system.

5. Conclusion

In the early 1920s, when Alvaro Obregón became president of Mexico and Warren G. Harding president of the United States, relations between the two governments were visibly strained. Over half a century later, the two countries have again inaugurated new presidents at roughly the same time. This time, however, the agenda of diplomatic dispute took a back seat to pronouncements of good will and neighborly intentions. Whereas in the earlier period Mexico was working out a revolution, one of whose purposes was the assertion of national sovereignty, in the mid-1970s Mexico was prepared to emphasize its dependence on the United States, in an effort to secure concessions from its northern neighbor.

Before World War II, conflicts between the U.S. and Mexico were highly visible and easily escalated. Diplomatic dispute with the U.S. posed a threat to Mexico's new found sense of national sovereignty, while from the U.S. perspective, the defense of an international economic and legal system was at stake. After the war, conflict was more often managed so as not to seriously disturb a relationship from which each side received some benefit. Mexico received capital from the United States, and it enjoyed most-favored nation status without formal obligations. The United States maintained profitable access to a politically stable, and cooperative neighbor, without massive security expense.

Despite the overwhelming military and economic superiority of the United States, diplomatic dispute between the two governments has been resolved at times to the greater advantage of Mexico. But this occasional power over conflict outcomes did not derive from conditions of complex interdependence, as described by Keohane and Nye. In the prewar period, Mexican power over outcomes was due to Mexican intransigence, born of internal conditions in Mexico in the aftermath of national revolution. U.S. reluctance to challenge this intransigence resulted from divisions within the U.S. government, and from considerations of collective U.S. interest as against the interest of particular investors in Mexico.

In the postwar period, some Mexican power over outcomes emerged from the international structure of relations between a world power and a dependent state. The Mexican government was more unified than the U.S. government, and paid greater attention to the conflicts, but these conditions did not suffice to explain occasional United States assent to postwar Mexican requests. Instead, Mexico's limited success derived from the U.S. desire, amid the trials of global leadership, to preserve political stability and to maintain an essentially cooperative relationship with its southern neighbor. For Mexico, this was a limited advantage indeed. For example, Mexican power was far more constrained and much less formidable than Canadian power, which was augmented by greater economic and political symmetry with the U.S., and by conditions of genuine complex interdependence.

Finally, a complete view of Mexico's power in diplomatic dispute with the United States must look beyond the record of conflict outcome. Many issues troublesome to Mexico never become conflicts on the U.S. presidential agenda. Mexico never seriously challenged American Cold War policies in the Western Hemisphere. It did not even raise extra-hemispheric political issues. Moreover, during the postwar period it did not initiate conflicts in an effort to escape its economic dependence on the U.S., and it never threatened to rupture close ties with its northern neighbor. Given the degree of Mexican economic dependence on the United States, this hesitant approach to diplomatic conflict was in some ways rational. Mexico did not challenge the U.S. in part because there were no substitutes for what the U.S. provided Mexico. But it suggests an element of self-denial as well. Mexican diplomats who contemplate greater independence from U.S. foreign policy are immediately cautioned by political realities in their own country. The Mexican private sector elite would make such a course of independence very costly for any Mexican administration that pursued it, quite apart from the reaction of the U.S. This is the full price of Mexico's structural dependence on the U.S.

It is possible that if Mexico associates with other nations in effective economic or political alliance, or if it finds substitutes for American capital, trade, and tourists, then its dependence on the U.S. would be reduced. Its diplomatic independence and its power over outcomes would increase. At present, however, Mexico is not actively seeking such substitutes, nor is it placing great emphasis on such alliances. Even as U.S. officials consider the virtues of a global approach to many of the problems in U.S.-Latin American relations, Mexico seems to have returned to its quest for a special bilateral relationship with the United States. If the past is at all prologue, the United States and Mexico will continue to relate as a world power and a dependent state, rather than as neighbors bound in global relations of complex interdependence.

NOTES

[1.] Jeffrey Hart distinguishes a third way of observing power, which is control over actors. For purposes of this essay , his conclusion is more important: that control over outcomes is the best way of observing power in action. "Three Approaches to the Measurement of Power in International Relations," *International Organization*, Vol. 30, No. 2 (Spring, 1976), pp. 289-305.

[2]Robert O. Keohane and Joseph S. Nye, Jr., *Power and Interdependence: World Politics in Transition* (Boston: Little, Brown and Company, 1977), pp. 24-29.

[3] *Ibid.*, chapter 7.

[4]This conclusion is tentative and information that contradicts it exists. One researcher found that the Mexican government's skill in manipulating the U.S. domestic policy-making process prevented the U.S. govern-

ment from becoming involved in a dispute with the Mexican government when the latter tightened the terms of an agreement with a U.S.-based sulphur company. The Mexicans may be able to keep potential conflicts off the agenda because of diplomatic skill and familiarity with the U.S. decision-making process, but that skill has not emerged in many of the presidential level conflicts. Cf. Theodore Moran, "Investor Disputes and the Structure of Constraints on U.S. Policy Formation," unpublished paper cited in Abraham F. Lowenthal, "Bureaucratic Politics and United States Policy Toward Latin America: An Interim Research Report," paper presented at the annual meeting of the American Political Science Association, 1974.

[5]Flavia Derossi, *The Mexican Entrepreneur* (Paris: Development Center of the Organization of Economic Co-operation and Development, 1971), pp. 76-87.

[6]José Luis Ceceña, *El Capital Monopolista y la Economía de México* (Mexico:Ediciones "El Caballito," 1963) cited in Lyle Brown and James Wilkie, "Recent United States-Mexican Relations: Problems Old and New," in John Braeman, et. al. (eds.), *Twentieth Century American Foreign Policy* (Columbus: Ohio State University Press, 1971), p. 411.

[7]*Latin America*, Vol. 10, No. 8 (February 20, 1976), p. 59.

[8]Roger Hansen, *The Politics of Mexican Development* (Baltimore: Johns Hopkins University Press, 1971), p. 66, and Clark Reynolds, *The Mexican Economy: Twentieth Century Structure and Growth* (New Haven: Yale University Press, 1970), pp. 235, 252.

[9]Benjamin Welles, "Travel Power: The Story Behind the Mexican Boycott," *New York Times*, June 27, 1976 and *Latin America*, Vol. 9. No. 50 (December 19, 1975), p. 393.

[10]Rafael Segovia, "El Nacionalismo Mexicano: Los Programas Políticos Revolucionarios, 1929-1964," *Foro Internacional*, Vol. 8, No. 4 (April-June, 1968), p. 356.

[11]Raymond Vernon, *The Dilemma of Mexico's Development: The Roles of the Private and Public Sectors* (Cambridge: Harvard University Press, 1963), pp. 94-95.

[12]Sanford Mosk argued the radical departure view in his *Industrial*

Revolution in Mexico (Berkeley: University of California Press, 1954), pp. 58-59; Robert Shafer supported a shift of emphasis interpretation in his *Mexico: Mutual Adjustment Planning* (Syracuse: Syracuse University Press, 1966), pp. 48-49.

[13]Reynolds, *loc. cit.*, p. 210 and Vernon, *loc. cit.*, p. 102.

[14]Olga Pellicer de Brody, "El Llamado a Las Inversiones Extranjeras, 1953-1958," in Bernado Sepúlveda Amor, et. al., *Las Empresas Transnacionales en México* (Mexico: El Colegio de México, 1974), pp. 75-104.

[15]Herbert K. May, *The Impact of Foreign Investment in Mexico* (New York: Council of the Americas, 1973), p. 23, and Richard S. Newfarmer and Willard F. Mueller, *Multinational Corporations in Brazil and Mexico: Structural Sources of Economic and Noneconomic Power,* A Report to the Subcommittee on Multinational Corporations of the Committee on Foreign Relations, U.S. Senate, 94th Cong., 1st Sess. (Washington: Government Printing Office, 1975), p. 62.

[16]May, *Ibid.*, p. 29; Newfarmer and Mueller, *Ibid.*, p. 50.

[17]Brown and Wilkie, *loc. cit.*, p. 414.

[18]See the sources listed at the bottom of Table 1.

[19]Hansen, *loc. cit.*, p. 170.

[20]Table 2 is based upon information that comes from numerous primary and secondary sources, the most useful of which were United States Department of State, *Foreign Relations of the United States* (Washington: Government Printing Office, 1920-1950); United States Department of State, *Department of State Bulletin* (Washington: Government Printing Office, various dates); National Archives and Records Service, *Public Papers of the Presidents of the United States* (Washington: Government Printing Office, various dates); Secretaría de Relaciones Exteriores, *Memorias de la Secretaría de Relaciones Exteriores* (México, 1920-1975); Presidencia de la República, *Informes de Presidentes de la República de México* (México, 1920-1975); Howard Cline, *The United States and Mexico,* rev. ed. (New York: Atheneum, 1963); Karl Schmitt, *Mexico and the United States, 1821-1973: Conflict and Coexistence* (New York: John Wiley & Sons, 1974); Luis G. Zorrilla,

Historia de las Relaciones Entre México y Los Estados Unidos, 1800-1953, (México: Editorial Porrua, 1965-1966).

[21]The names of the issue areas that appear in Table 2 were adapted from those used by Keohane and Nye, *Power and Interdependence*, Chapter 7, to describe the areas within which the U.S.-Canadian and U.S.-Australian conflicts fell, i.e. politico-military, diplomatic, socio-economic, joint resource problems, and competing sovereignty claims. Later in this paper we shall discuss trade conflicts as though they belong in a separate issue area; for now, however, they are included in the general socio-economic issue area. Table 2 actually understates the importance of economic matters to the U.S.-Mexican conflict agenda. For one thing, the two prewar diplomatic conflicts arose because of contemporary economic disagreements; for another thing, some of the postwar conflicts in other issue areas (e.g., the joint resource salinity and fisheries disputes) became conflicts because of their economic importance.

[22]Support for this point may be inferred from a recent essay in which David Ronfeldt, one of the more astute observers of Mexican military affairs, did not include defense of the country from external aggressors as a source of the military's political influence or even as an important function. "The Mexican Army and Political Order Since 1940," in James Wilkie, et. al. (eds.), *Contemporary Mexico: Papers of the IV International Congress of Mexican History* (Berkeley: University of California Press, 1976), pp. 317-336.

[23]Hart, *loc. cit.*, p. 292.

[24]*Ibid.*

[25]The Cuban Revolution as a problem for Mexican policy is the subject of Olga Pellicer de Brody, *México y la Revolución Cubana*, (Mexico: El Colego de México, 1972), and Arthur K. Smith, Jr., *Mexico and the Cuban Revolution: Foreign Policy-Making in Mexico under President Adolfo Lopez Mateos, 1958-1964*, Ph.D. dissertation, Cornell University, 1974.

[26]It is difficult to determine the intensity of presidential involvement in the postwar conflicts from the available published materials. For example, President Eisenhower wrote to Secretary of State Dulles in June 1955, "I probably have written to you more on the subject of Mexico

than any other single matter....I am so earnestly of the opinion that our relations with Mexico must be a first and continuing concern of ours..." But, other published evidence does not suggest that Mexico was a constant concern of either the president or of his secretary of state. Dwight D. Eisenhower, *The White House Years: Waging Peace, 1956-1961* (Garden City: Doubleday, 1965), pp. 517n-518n.

[27]On the attitudes of elite groups, business organizations, and various Mexican administrations toward foreign investment, see *Mexican Elite Attitudes toward Foreign Investment* (Washington: United States Information Agency, Office of Research, May 1974); Robert J. Shafer, *Mexican Business Organizations: History and Analysis* (Syracuse: Syracuse University Press, 1973); Alexander Bohrisch and Wolfgang Konig, *La Política Mexicana Sobre Inversiónes Extranjeras* (México: El Colegio de México, 1968).

[28]John Womack, Jr., "The Spoils of the Mexican Revolution," *Foreign Affairs*, Vol. 48, No. 4 (July, 1970), p. 681.

[29]See Miguel Wionczek, *El Nacionalismo Mexicano y la Inversión Extrajera, 3rd ed.* (Mexico: Siglo XXI, 1975).

[30]*New York Times*, November 24, 1972.

[31]Frank Brandenburg, *The Making of Modern Mexico* (Englewood Cliffs: Prentice-Hall, Inc., 1964), p. 318. A description of the formal arrangements and constitutional authority for the conduct of Mexican foreign policy can be found in Antonio Gonzales de León, "¿Quién Administra Las Relaciones Internacionales de México?", *Relaciones Internacionales* II: 4 (January-March, 1974), pp. 5-27.

[32]Norris Hundley, Jr., *Dividing the Waters: A Century of Controversy Between the United States and Mexico* (Berkeley: University of California Press, 1966).

[33]Richard B. Craig, *The Bracero Program: Interest Groups and Foreign Policy* (Austin: University of Texas Press, 1971).

[34]*Foreign Relations of the United States*, 1948, Vol. IX, pp. 606-610.

[35]Hundley, *loc. cit.*

[36]Craig, *loc. cit.*, pp. 102-125.

[37]*Foreign Relations of the United States*, 1921, Vol. II, pp. 397-404.

[38]Historian Dana Munro wrote that Mexican president Plutarco Elías Calles agreed to aid the Nicaraguan Liberals in exchange for Liberal leader Juan Sacasa's promise to abrogate a canal treaty with the United States once the Liberals were in office. *The United States and the Caribbean Republics, 1921-1933* (Princeton: Princeton University Press, 1974), p. 200. On the Coolidge speech see James Horn, "Did the United States Plan an invasion of Mexico in 1927?", *Journal of Interamerican Studies and World Affairs*, Vol. 15, No. 4 (November, 1973), p. 455.

[39]The postwar conflict over oil is the subject of an essay by Lorenzo Meyer, "La Resistencia al Capital Privado Extranjero: El Caso Del Petroleo, 1938-1950," in Bernardo Sepúlveda Amor, et. al., *Las Empresas Transnacionales*, pp. 107-156. Meyer's essay is the only published account of the important negotiations between Mexico and the United States in the postwar period. It is this writer's interpretation, based upon a reading of the *Foreign Relations of the United States* (1945-1950) and the presidential papers for the Truman years, that Meyer did not give sufficient weight to Truman's hostility toward the oil giants and to his concern for economic stability in Mexico as an aspect of the negotiations, but the most recent volumes in the *Foreign Relations* series probably were not available when the Meyer essay was written.

[40]This notion of hegemony is taken from Jorge I. Domínguez, *The U.S. Impact on Cuban Internal Politics and Economics, 1902-1958: From Imperialism to Hegemony.* Paper delivered at the 1976 Annual Meeting of the American Political Science Association.

[41]*Comercio Exterior*, June, 1969, p.2.

[42]This section was based upon E. David Cronon, *Josephus Daniels in Mexico* (Madison: University of Wisconsin Press, 1960); *Foreign Relations of the United States;* Lorenzo Meyer, *México y los Estados Unidos en el Conflicto Petrolero, 1917-1942*, 2nd ed. (Mexico: El Colegio de México, 1972); and Bryce Wood, *The Making of the Good Neighbor Policy* (New York: W.W. Norton, 1961).

[43]Quoted in Wood, *Ibid.*, p. 250.

[44]*Foreign Relations of the United States*, 1938, Vol. V, pp. 729-733.

[45]I.A. Litvak and C.J. Maule, "Foreign Investment in Mexico: Some Lessons for Canada," *Behind the Headlines*, The Canadian Institute of International Affairs, Vol. 30, Nos. 5-6 (July, 1971), p. 13.

[46]Cline, *loc. cit.*, p. 2.

[47]The data on Canada is taken from Joseph S. Nye, Jr., "Transnational Relations and Interstate Conflicts: An Empirical Analysis," *International Organization*, Vol. 28, No. 4 (Autumn, 1974), pp. 961-996.

[48]Nye did not distinguish trade as a separate issue area. Coding judgements about U.S.-Canadian trade conflicts are this author's responsibility.

[49]See, for example, Martin C. Needler, *Politics and Society in Mexico* (Albuquerque: University of New Mexico Press, 1971), pp. 46-48.

[50]For one interpretation and review of Echeverría's foreign policy see Errol D. Jones and David Lafrance, "Mexico's Foreign Affairs under President Luis Echeverría: The Special Case of Chile," *Inter-American Economic Affairs*, Vol. 30, No. 1 (Summer, 1976), pp. 45-78.

[51]Two cogent discussions of the economic dimensions of Mexican foreign policy during the Echeverría administration are Olga Pellicer de Brody, "Mexico in the 1970s and its Relations with the United States," in Julio Cotler and Richard R. Fagen (eds.), *Latin America and the United States: The Changing Political Realities* (Stanford: Stanford University Press, 1974), pp. 314-333 and her "Cambios Recientes en la Política Exterior de México," in Centro de Estudios Internacionales, *La Política Exterior de México: Realidad y Perspectivas* (México: El Colegio de México, 1972), pp. 39-54.

[52]*Business Latin America*, March 2, 1977, p. 70.

[53]*Ibid.*, January 26, 1977, p. 25.

[54]For historiography and a review of some of the materials pertinent to the subject see Arthur F. Corwin, "Mexican Emigration History, 1900-1970: Literature and Research," *Latin American Research Review*, Vol. VIII, No. 2 (Summer, 1973), pp. 3-24.

[55]One scholar argues sensibly that because of the "clandestine nature of the population and its great geographic dispersion through the United States, it is impossible to estimate the size of the total illegal population with any degree of precision, using any extant source of data." Wayne A. Cornelius, *Illegal Mexican Migration to the United States: A Summary of Research Findings and Policy Implications* (Cambridge, Massachusetts: M.I.T. Center of International Studies, Migration and Development Monograph Series, 1977), p. 1.

[56]Francisco Alba-Hernández, "Exodo Silencioso: la Emigración de Trabajadores Mexicanos a Estados Unidos," *Foro Internacional*, Vol. 17, No. 2 (Oct.-Dec., 1976), p. 155.

[57]Cornelius, *loc. cit.*, p. 4.

[58]"On the Problem of Illegal Mexican Aliens." Excerpts from the U.S. Comptroller-General's report of October 19, 1976, entitled *Immigration: Need to Reassess U.S. Policy*, reprinted in *Inter-American Economic Affairs*, Vol. 30, No. 3 (Winter, 1976), p. 96.

[59]Cornelius, *loc. cit.*, pp. 3-5.

[60]*Ibid.*, p. 14.

[61]*Ibid.*, p. 15.

[62]*Ibid.*, p. 16.

[63]See, for instance, *Illegal Aliens*, Hearings before Subcommittee No. 1 of the Committee on the Judiciary, House of Representatives, 92nd Cong., 2nd Sess., (Washington: Government Printing Office, 1973).

[64]For an example of a warning which predicts unfortunate results from several proposed plans to deal with the problem of illegal aliens, see "Mexican Says U.S. Invites Disaster on Illegal Aliens," *New York Times*, May 26, 1977.

[65]On Mexico's position toward OPEC see *Business Week*. October 26, 1974; *Latin America*, Vol. IX, No. 2 (January 10, 1975) and Vol. IX, No. 3 (January 17, 1975); *Latin American Economic Report*, Vol. III, No. 47 (November, 1975). The U.S. threat of trade sanctions is reported in *Le Monde*, May 21, 1976.

[66]*Latin American Economic Review*, Vol. V, No. 2 (January 14, 1977), p. 8.

[67]*Ibid.*, Vol. 9 (March 4, 1977), p. 35.

[68]Predictions are that the present production of 1,603,507 barrels per day (BPD) will rise to 2,240,000 BPD, while exports of crude and refined products would increase from 153,000 BPD to 1,105,000 BPD. *Ibid.*

CONCLUSION:
CONFLICT AND INTERDEPENDENCE
IN U.S. FOREIGN POLICY

Robert L. Paarlberg

CONTENTS

CONCLUSION:
CONFLICT AND INTERDEPENDENCE
IN U.S. FOREIGN POLICY

Robert L. Paarlberg

These three studies of past U.S. relations with Iran, Japan, and Mexico stand by themselves as separate investigations into the dynamic of diplomatic dispute under changing conditions. But by similarity of research design, and for reasons presented in the introduction to this volume, they also invite comparison. Accordingly, the major findings from these three cases are reviewed and compared here. They are compared first to one another, and then to findings from the earlier Keohane-Nye study of U.S. relations with Canada and with Australia. This comparative effort will include a restatement of where "complex interdependence" was or was not observed in these three new cases, a review of how the three conflict agendas under study came to be formed, and then some explanation of similar and dissimilar patterns of conflict resolution. Finally, all of the conflict histories under consideration here will be viewed with special reference to the one variable which they hold in common—the uncertain future conduct of U.S. foreign policy.

1. The Missing Conditions of Complex Interdependence

The U.S. Ambassador to Canada, Thomas O. Enders, recently argued that U.S. relations with Canada constitute "an advance model of the relationships which will exist in the 21st century between all the industrial democracies. Everywhere—Europe, Japan, America—you find countries being drawn together in the same way... In this regard Canada and the U.S. are like the rest... only more so."

These studies provide little evidence to support such a conclusion. By the close of the half century under review, the U.S. did find itself in some ways "interdependent" with Mexico, Iran, and Japan. But in no case did this interdependence approximate the ideal type defined by Keohane and Nye as "complex interdependence," specifically observed in the case of U.S. relations with Canada. And in every case, including the industrial democratic case of Japan, further evolution toward conditions of complex interdependence was judged to be at best problematic.

In the major case study of U.S. relations with Mexico, some of the conditions of "complex interdependence" were indeed satisfied. Certainly the presence or employment of armed forces did play a negligible role in U.S.-Mexican relations. Military security issues not only failed to dominate the bilateral conflict agenda, they scarcely appeared on that agenda. But, this did not mean that "issue hierarchies" were missing in the Mexican case. Trade and other socio-economic matters simply dominated politico-military and diplomatic matters, rather than the other way around. Also, multiple points of transnational and transgovernmental contact were found between the U.S. and Mexico. Yet these contacts were lacking in symmetry, so much that they contributed more to a relationship of "dependence" than to one of ideal "complex interdependence." Mexico did not enjoy so many channels of access to the U.S. business community and to the U.S. Government as the U.S. enjoyed channels of access to Mexico. Mexican officials experienced much more difficulty than their Canadian counterparts in making effective contact with the various centers of decision-making power within the American bureaucracy. Finally, transnational trade and money flows between the U.S. and Mexico were of differing value to the two nations. Trade with Mexico today constitutes only four percent of the U.S. overseas total, while trade with the U.S. accounts for more than sixty percent of Mexico's total overseas commerce.

In the case of U.S. relations with Japan, a true "reciprocal dependence" has developed within some important issue areas, including money and trade. By 1975, Japan had grown to become the third largest economic power in the world, and second behind Canada as a U.S. trading partner. Roughly twenty-five percent of Japan's $120 billion annual foreign commerce was shared with the U.S. But commerce alone does not constitute a fully developed state of complex interdependence. The substantial U.S. trade with Japan actually takes place against a background of very little direct transgovernmental contact and private multinational investment. As late as 1973, most Japanese industries remained closed by law to majority foreign ownership. Even with the more recent liberalization of these restrictions, U.S. direct investment in Japan has grown to little more than three percent of the U.S. overseas total. And Japanese foreign direct investment in the U.S. still accounts for a mere one percent of the total, compared to twenty percent for Canada, and fifty-three percent for the European Economic Community.

So Japan remains at "arm's length" from many of the internal structures of the U.S. economy, and *vice versa.* Transgovernmental ties between the two countries are also limited in number, and were found in the textile dispute to be of limited policy significance. Language, race, and geographic distance all restrict the rapid development of these transnational and transgovernmental ties which are necessary for further evolution toward full conditions of complex interdependence.

It is also important, in the Japanese case, that a skewed distribution of military capabilities and a unilateral U.S. security guarantee influence the conduct of day-to-day conflict relations, much more than in either the Mexican or the Canadian case. Japan, which still spends less than one percent of its GNP on its military forces, remains heavily and conspicuously reliant upon this U.S. security guarantee. Such guarantees may not be taken for granted by Japan, so much as by contiguous Mexico or Canada, or even some allied states in Western Europe. Japan must forever temper its U.S. policies with a "realist" concern for security protection. In this critical respect, Japan again falls well short of the Canadian example of "complex interdependence."

In the case of Iran, traditional security concerns also remained critical to the daily foreign policy calculations of the two governments. Even in a period of reduced Cold War tensions, the U.S. still valued Iran primarily as a source of security and stability in the Persian Gulf, where British forces have now been largely withdrawn. Beyond its obvious commercial value, even Iranian oil was valued as a critical security asset for America's European allies and for an increasingly isolated Isreal. Iran's preoccupation with security matters was even more obvious. Alliance relations with the U.S. and the heavy conventional arms trade were seen as critical means to gain regional strength and to recover some of the traditional glories of ancient Imperial Persia. Military security issues may be out of fashion elsewhere, but they continued to structure the conduct of foreign relations between the U.S. and Iran.

Multiple channels of transnational and transgovernmental contact were certainly not missing from the Iranian case. But these channels, until recently, were instruments of Iran's "dependence" rather than a feature of genuine "interdependence." Foreign agents, foreign companies, foreign advisers, foreign aid—these transnational activities were long employed by Britain and by the U.S. as means to contain and to compromise Iranian sovereignty. Iran has now escaped from most of these structures of transnational dependence, and has increased its sovereign control over external contacts. But by doing so it actually retards the growth of reciprocal structures of genuine complex interdependence.

So all three of these new bilateral cases fall short of fully developed complex interdependence. If we can imagine a spectrum of bilateral relations, from perfect realism at one extreme to perfect complex interdependence at the other, U.S. relations with Mexico and with Japan certainly fall closer to complex interdependence than do relations with Iran and with Australia. But none falls so close to complex interdependence as in the exceptional case of U.S. relations with Canada:

Figure 1. Comparison of Conflict Relations, 1975

1. Unified nation states dominant actors	1. Important actors other than unified states
2. Armed forces an important instrument of policy	2. Armed forces an unimportant policy instrument
3. Issues arranged in hierarchical fashion	3. No clear division between high politics and low politics issues

As a summarizing device, this simple spectrum of relations has obvious drawbacks. Notice, for example, that along this single dimension, U.S.-Mexican relations fall closer to complex interdependence than do U.S.-Japanese relations. This is because of the intimate transnational and border contacts which connect Mexico so closely with the U.S. But this study has confirmed that Mexico's relationship to the U.S. is otherwise *unlike* the Canadian example of complex interdependence, because of *asymmetric* economic flows across the common border and because of dependent attitudes and limited objectives held by Mexican elites. To emphasize this important difference between the Mexican and the Japanese case it is necessary to add another dimension to the simple horizontal scheme considered here, a vertical dimension of relative "dependence." Perfect "dependence" may be defined for our purpose as an *asymmetry* in transnational flows, organizational contacts, and national capabilities, or preceived capabilities, which renders *only one state* in a bilateral relationship *vulnerable to a termination of those flows or contracts, or to a use of those capabilities.*[1] The opposite condition of perfect "symmetry" (be it mutual vulnerability, or mutual invulnerability) does not leave only one state exclusively dependent upon the other. When this new vertical dimension of symmetry-dependence is added to the horizontal dimension of realism-complex interdependence, the five bilateral relations under review may be placed in a more appropriate position relative to one another:

Figure 2. Symmetry and Dependence in Conflict Relations, 1975

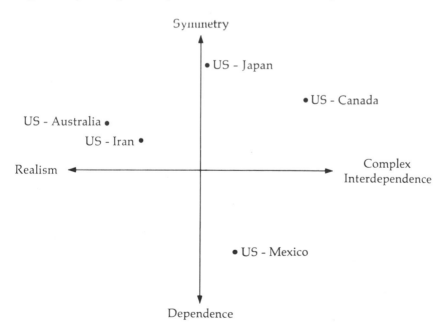

On this two-dimensional field the true position of U.S.-Mexican relations relative to those with Canada or Japan comes more clearly into view. Mexico still falls to the right of Japan, but much lower and closer to the pole of "dependence" than to either "realism" or "complex interdependence."[2] Japan, by virtue of the greater symmetry in its economic relations with the U.S., assumes a true position which is now more nearly "Canadian." Also, Iran shows just enough lingering "dependence" upon the U.S. to fall somewhat away from its earlier close proximity to Japan. (If some member states of the European Community were to be added to this field, their relationship to the U.S. would very likely fall almost as far to the right as Canada, in the direction of "complex interdependence," and yet even higher, closer to "symmetry" than the case of Canada.)

Looking to the future, it is probable that Mexico will move upward on this field, just as Iran had moved upward by 1975 to escape its more dependent position of the past. Mexico's newly discovered petroleum wealth is likely to speed this process, as did Iran's own oil wealth.

But it seems less likely that either Mexico, Iran, or even Japan will move much further to the right, toward the pole of "complex interdependence" with the U.S. Whatever the size of its newfound petroleum reserves, Mexico will not soon enjoy the advanced economic standing of a Canada, and it will never enjoy the tie of common culture and language so critical to Canada's interdependent relations with the U.S.

In the Iranian case, geographic as well as cultural distance retards the growth of reciprocal transnational contact. The U.S., by sending its businessmen to Iran, by educating so many Iranian students, and by training so many Iranian military personnel, many of whom later became top level policy makers, did enjoy some multi-channel access to Tehran. And Iranian officials have at least done better than the Mexicans or the Japanese in direct dealings with some parts of the U.S. business community or the U.S. government bureaucracy. But Iran's informal access to the U.S. will continue to fall far short of that noted in the Canadian case.

And finally, in the case of Japan, racial and more difficult language differences add further barriers to any evolution toward full complex interdependence with the U.S. Keohane and Nye observed that geographic distance alone was enough to block the growth of transsocietal contact in the U.S.-Australian case, where race and language were not an impediment to such contact.[3] Despite a strong economic attraction between the U.S. and Japan, and despite some advanced industrial cultural convergence, inter-societal interaction between the two countries will not soon grow to approximate the U.S.-Canada standard. The Japanese remain concerned that foreign economic activities within their country might introduce "alien" marketing, finance, or employment practices. And Americans, for their part, remain equally sensitive to Japanese economic activities within the U.S. Formal barriers to interaction can and have been reduced. But informal and geographic limits to inter-societal penetration will remain.

Nor can one dismiss the continued future importance of armed forces in U.S.-Japanese and U.S.-Iranian relations. In the Japanese case, the U.S. security guarantee remains critical to the conduct of Japan's foreign and domestic policies. And for Iran, its rapidly growing military capabilities portend anything but a negligible role for armed forces in the future of Iranian foreign relations.

So a conclusion may be drawn that U.S.-Canadian relations are not "an advance model" of relationships which will soon develop between the U.S. and Mexico, Iran, or even Japan. As Keohane and Nye concede, Canada is more likely to prove an advance model for U.S. interdependence with certain industrial nations of Western Europe, such as Great Britain or the Federal Republic of Germany. But any hope that U.S. relations with nations beyond the North Atlantic community can soon evolve to approximate the Canadian example seems to be misplaced.

One important observation fits with and follows from the failure of these three new cases to fully satisfy conditions of "complex interdependence." In none of these three cases did transnational organizations, such as multinational business corporations, play a large role in the creation or generation of interstate conflict. In the Canadian case, where conditions of complex interdependence were most clearly satisfied, ten of the thirty-one high-level conflicts noted after 1950 did involve transnational organizations.[4] But in the Japanese case, only three of fifteen postwar cases showed transnational organization involvement. In the case of Iran, despite the high visibility of oil issues on the agenda, transnational organizations were involved in only four of eleven postwar conflict cases, as opposed to six of eleven cases before 1945. And in the Mexican case, only two of fifteen postwar cases featured such involvement. Mexico, although an important target for U.S. direct investment, showed as little transnational organization involvement in the creation of conflict as did distant Australia.

In each of these three new cases, the agenda setting role of trans-national organizations appeared to be not only low, but acutally in decline. In the Mexican case and in the Iranian case, this decline was observed even with regard to the activities of the large and otherwise powerful U.S.-based international oil companies. In the Japanese case, this decline was somewhat less dramatic, in part because the agenda-setting role of transnational organizations between the U.S. and Japan had never been very high.[5]

But the failure of these three new cases to fully satisfy the standards of "complex interdependence" fails to account for two important aspects of the bilateral activity under review here. First, despite a weak role for multinationals in conflict creation, and despite the continuing importance of armed force in these bilateral relations, "economic" issues nonetheless found their way, consistently, to the top of all three conflict agendas. And second, conflict resolution often favored the immediate objectives of the "weaker" power. In these two respects the conflict relations explored here come close to satisfying the *expectations* of a complex interdependent relationship without having satisfied all of the *pre-conditions* of complex interdependence. This discovery calls for extended discussion and explanation.

2. Unexpected Patterns of Conflict Agenda Formation

Despite an absence of complex interdependence with the U.S., all three nations, Mexico, Japan, and Iran, found themselves in day-to-day conflict with the U.S. over socio-economic issues much of the time, or even most of the time. In the Japanese case, fourteen out of all thirty conflicts since 1920 dealt with socio-economic or joint resource issues. During the postwar period, this ratio increased to nine out of fifteen. In the Iranian case, ten out of twenty-two conflicts were socio-economic conflicts, including five of eleven since 1945. And in the Mexican case, seventeen out of all twenty-two conflicts were socio-economic or trade conflicts. If joint resource conflicts are included in this last total, then the U.S.-Mexican conflict agenda since 1920 actually contains only three high-level conflicts out of twenty-two which did *not* focus primarily upon economic issues or objectives. This Mexican case shows a prepon-derance of socio-economic conflict even greater than that encountered in the Canadian case, in which twenty-two of thirty-nine high level conflicts were socio-economic or joint resource issues. So it must be concluded that complex interdependence is not a necessary condition for the high agenda status of economic or social conflict,[6] even in bilateral relations with the U.S., a nation which has often been described as preoccupied with security affairs during the postwar period. This great visibility of socio-economic conflict might have been expected prior to

World War II, when the business of America was business, and when foreign policies in the Pacific and the Caribbean in particular were geared to the promotion and protection of American enterprise. But during the postwar period, supposedly a Cold War era of intense security preoccupation, it is striking to discover so many socio-economic issues at the top of the conflict agenda. Several observations will help to explain this phenomenon.

First, it seems that the Cold War era has come to be remembered incorrectly as devoid of economic concerns for U.S. foreign policy.[7] This was not only an era of security crises in Berlin, Korea, Cuba, or Vietnam. It was also an era of the Marshall Plan, of Third World development aid, and of unprecedented U.S. leadership in global trade and monetary arrangements. Second, some of the conflicts coded as "economic" conflicts in this study deserve to be counted as politico-military conflicts at the same time. This is certainly the case with the Iranian oil conflicts of the 1950s. Third, politico-military objectives surely *did* dominate U.S. postwar conflict relations with rival powers such as the Soviet Union and China, and with "endangered" allies such as Korea, South Vietnam, or Israel. But the three nations considered in this study include neither a prominent postwar rival, nor a particularly endangered postwar client or ally.

But a fourth and less obvious explanation is as important as these first three. Potential politico-military conflicts with Mexico, Japan, and Iran often failed to reach the agenda because they were effectively resolved at a higher "structural" level, a level of unchallenged U.S. military preponderance and unchanging security alliance. During the postwar era, the U.S. was so far beyond effective politico-military challenge from any of these three weaker nations that security questions seldom arose.

This final explanation for the low visibility of politico-military conflict is best illustrated by the issue of Vietnam, which was never raised by Mexico, Japan, or Iran to the status of a high-level conflict with the U.S. By a rule of anticipated reaction, none of these three states saw reason to create a sensitive conflict, which they could not hope to win, over Indochina. In the Japanese case, a high-level conflict over Vietnam was never formally initiated despite Japan's unconcealed domestic objections to the U.S. bombing policy in Southeast Asia. In the Mexican case, a similar reluctance prevailed, not just on Vietnam, but also with regard to other "objectionable" U.S. security policies in the Dominican Republic and in Cuba. Iran's possible objections to U.S. policy in Indochina were also cautiously withheld. In Iran's case, this forbearance from criticizing U.S. activities in Southeast Asia brought grateful concessions from the U.S. on non-security issues, such as oil prices, which Iran considered to be more important.

In any case, a preponderance of socio-economic conflict need not follow from conditions described earlier as complex interdependence, or from the behavior of transnational organizations which contribute to conflict creation under such conditions. In these three new bilateral cases, a high visibility of socio-economic conflict and a low visibility of politico-military conflict were found within the traditional context of alliance relations.

3. Unexpected Patterns of Conflict Outcome

As with conflict creation, so with conflict resolution. The patterns of resolution observed in this study were somewhat unexpected. In all three cases the "weaker" state managed at times to secure conflict outcomes more favorable to its own immediate objectives. In the Keohane-Nye study of U.S.-Canadian conflict, this same pattern of conflict resolution was noticed during the postwar period, and was attributed, in part, to the diminished role of traditional power assets under modern conditions of "complex interdependence." But in the three conflict cases considered here, the conditions of complex interdependence were not fully satisfied. Instead, U.S. conflict outcomes with Mexico, Japan, and Iran have often favored the weaker party precisely because the U.S. was willing, and strong enough, to have it that way. In order to pursue larger global objectives, Washington often found it convenient to offer some marginal bilateral advantage to its junior partners and clients. The U.S. was not only strong enough to set the rules which governed its relations with these three smaller states, it was also strong enough to set non-coercive rules, which are the most efficient means to preserve the smooth conduct of alliance politics.

The U.S. first established its "rule-making" power over Japan by force of arms, in 1945, and over Iran by means of covert intervention, in 1953. But in both cases it then went on to preserve that power by a more benevolent technique, by offering a tangible advantage in patterns of day-to-day conflict outcome to these same allied or client states which it had taken by force into its sphere of influence.

These marginal advantages in conflict outcome were not extended to all allied states in equal measure. Iran has clearly done best of the three considered here. Although a U.S. client, the Shah learned to enjoy an advantage in day-to-day conflict relations with the U.S., first by threatening to weaken his alliance, and later by playing upon his contribution to that alliance. In five conflict cases out of seven noted after 1953, outcomes fell closer to the objectives of Iran than to those of the U.S. Before Iran had become a U.S. client state, the U.S. had enjoyed a relative advantage in nine conflicts out of fifteen.

Japan's postwar record of conflict with the U.S. is not so clearly weighted to its own advantage. But even as a thoroughly defeated power after 1945, Japan did secure an outcome closer to its own objective in six of fifteen postwar conflicts. And in the 1960s, before the period of the "Nixon shocks" of 1971, five out of six conflict outcomes favored Japan. In fact, Washington's harsh treatment of Japan in 1971 was in many ways a corrective to the highly favorable position which Japan enjoyed prior to 1971.

Japan was neither able nor inclined to manipulate its security alliance with the U.S. to such effect as Iran. Nonetheless, early during the postwar period it managed to resist U.S. pressures to share the burden of that relationship and it was finally able to gain a favorable security treaty revision, even while it prospered from nearly $2 billion in U.S. assistance toward its own economic revival. Since Japan was always recognized at face value by the U.S. as a potential industrial superpower critical to the conduct of Pacific security affairs, it did not have to "pledge loyalty" or "threaten disloyalty," like Iran, to gain special consideration from the U.S. The U.S. was prepared, on its own initiative, to underwrite Japan's economic recovery and to respond to some of Japan's political needs in order to preserve security interests in the Pacific area. In 1970, when Japan's security treaty with the U.S. was again extended, an official Japanese statement gave recognition to this important bilateral advantage: "The fact that Japan enjoys peace, unprecedented economic prosperity, and improvement of the people's livelihood, amid a violently unsettled international situation, shows that the country made the right national choice on the course of its foreign policy."

Even Mexico, despite its dependence upon the U.S. during the postwar period, secured conflict outcomes more favorable or equally favorable to its own objectives in eight out of fifteen cases. Perhaps more telling, ten of these fifteen postwar cases dealt with matters predominantly under U.S. jurisdiction. Only one of seven prewar conflicts had occurred within areas of predominant U.S. jurisdiction. Even when Mexico did not gain favorable conflict outcomes during the postwar period, it at least managed to shift the venue of conflict away from Mexican national sovereignty or Mexican resources, and toward U.S. policies, and in some cases, U.S. resources.

We might speculate that Mexico would have done even better in its postwar relations with the U.S. if it could have pushed some high-level security concerns onto the conflict agenda. Perhaps if Mexico had raised stronger objections to U.S. policy toward Cuba, the Dominican Republic, or Indochina, it could have developed "bargaining chips" to trade away in non-security dealings with the U.S. Japan and Iran held such bargaining chips without effort, owing to their more critical geographic position, adjacent to Soviet spheres of influence. But Mexico, as an insulated hemispheric state, experienced great difficulty in raising credible threats of "independence" from the U.S. on matters of security. Its proximity to the U.S. and its much greater sense of dependence stunted its diplomatic activities, at least until the very end of the period here under review. Bargaining skills can make a difference in bilateral relations. But no diplomatic sleight of hand could have given to Mexico the postwar diplomatic leverage of Japan or Iran.[9]

4. Joint Gains in Postwar Relations with the U.S.

Japan, Iran, Mexico, and the U.S. have not always enjoyed mutually advantageous bilateral relations. Particularly before World War II, each of these three bilateral relationships was marked by failure to secure joint gains. Recall that the Iranian government had been unable to reach a mutually profitable accommodation with the U.S. business community or with the U.S. State Department, owing to objections from Britain and from the Soviet Union. Regardless of whether the U.S. or Iran tended to prevail in conflict relations at this point, neither had reason to be pleased with the relationship. Only after 1941, and more clearly after 1953, did Iranian and American leaders find themselves able to deal directly with one another on a mutually advantageous basis. Relations between the two were no longer encumbered by the need to satisfy British or Soviet interests. The Iranian government had to sacrifice some of its early nationalist ambition to function effectively in this way, as a subservient client of the U.S. But the diplomatic strength and ambition of Iran today is in part a product of this earlier sacrifice.

Likewise, U.S. relations with Japan before 1945 were decidedly disadvantageous to both nations. The outbreak and the conduct of the costly war in the Pacific gave final expression to this condition of mutual disadvantage. Not until the Japanese surrender (and again, initially on U.S. terms) were conditions finally suited to a close and profitable U.S.-Japanese alliance. Japan promptly became a part of the "free world," its economy was revived under a benevolent regime of U.S. trade and assistance, and visible gains in security and prosperity came to dominate the experience of both parties in the relationship.

Although to a lesser degree, Mexican-American relations were also governed to greater mutual advantage after the war than before the war. As U.S. diplomacy became heavily engaged beyond Latin America after 1945, it is true that Mexico suffered some relative neglect, particularly as a recipient of direct economic assistance. But this neglect was in some ways advantageous to Mexico. Recall that none of the postwar U.S.-Mexican conflicts matched the intensity of those of the prewar era. For some in Mexico, this postwar pattern of U.S. distraction promised the best of two worlds—a security guarantee without reciprocal obligation, and no revival of the intense U.S. political interest in Mexican resource or sovereignty questions, such as those which plagued relations during the prewar era. After 1945, Mexico may have been "no closer to God and no farther from the U.S.," but the expansive energies of U.S. diplomacy were now safely engaged in matters far beyond the hemisphere.

So there was some reason for all three of these states to prefer their postwar experience in dealings with the U.S. to their prewar experience. The postwar expansion of U.S. diplomacy has not fallen kindly on all nations, to say the least. But those considered here, once allied with U.S. Cold War policy, whether from choice or necessity, did find some of their diplomatic circumstances improved.

And again, these advantages enjoyed by Japan, Iran, and Mexico were not one-sided. The extension of modest benefits to these allied states in each case made it easier for the U.S. to maintain its global Cold War alliance system. By paying the costs of system maintenance, the U.S. received considerable benefits of its own.

In the case of Mexico, for example, the U.S. continued to avoid the burden of offering any special concessions to Mexican trade, even while it enjoyed the unequal benefit which grew from a dominant position in that trade. In the Japanese case, beyond the matter of trade relations, the U.S. was able to secure extended use of Japanese territories in its maintenance of Pacific security. And through postwar ties to Iran, the U.S. maintained an anti-communist ally on the very borders of the Soviet Union, and found a means to provide some stability in the Persian Gulf following the departure of British forces. On balance, the U.S. suffered little, if at all, from the benefits which it initially extended to its postwar allies.

5. The Threat to Mutually Advantageous Bilateral Relations

As Cold War tensions have relaxed, this mutually advantageous aspect of U.S. relations with Iran, Japan, and Mexico has been somewhat modified. Following a fourfold increase in OPEC oil prices, undertaken largely at the insistence of Iran, Washington's tolerant view of the Shah as a faithful friend came under increasing strain. In the Far East, trade and money disputes, combined with the eventual demise of U.S. military pretensions in Southeast Asia and a surprise U.S. opening to China, shifted the foundation of U.S. policy toward Japan. The U.S. momentarily felt disinclined to carry the full burden of Pacific security. Finally, outspoken Mexican diplomatic support for a new international economic order to improve the lot of poor nations, at the expense of some longstanding advantages enjoyed by the rich, also placed a strain upon U.S. relations with its neighbor to the south.

Keohane and Nye demonstrate that mutually advantageous relations, under conditions of "complex interdependence," can develop the strength to survive such strain, even in the face of nationalist tendencies toward adjustment for short-term unilateral advantage. For example, the regime which governed U.S.-Canadian relations during the postwar period discouraged tactics of overt "issue linkage," or the attempt to refuse concessions on one conflict until reciprocating concessions have been received on another. When Canadian economic nationalism developed in the late 1960s and early 1970s, some in the U.S. advocated that new tariffs or taxes be "linked" to Canadian policies, as one means to check the Canadian challenge. But, observe Keohane and Nye, the politics of "complex interdependence" discouraged the U.S. from employing such linkage tactics. Too many domestic interests in the U.S. with separate ties to Canada and with a separate stake in the Canadian-American relationship stood in the way of this strategy. Transnational and transgovernmental contacts between the U.S. and Canada had become so extensive and so complex that they could not easily be altered by a crude strategy of *quid pro quo*, even by political leaders who may have wished to employ such a strategy. So the joint gains which stood to be realized from an ongoing U.S.-Canadian regime of "quiet diplomacy" survived this period of momentary disadvantage for the U.S.[10]

Where conditions of complex interdependence are not so well established, constraints against tactics of "issue linkage" may not be so durable as in the Canadian case. We have seen here that complete structures of complex interdependence have not yet developed between the U.S. and Mexico, the U.S. and Iran, or even between the U.S. and

Japan. From this observation, one might expect the Canadian example not to apply in U.S. relations with Mexico, Japan, and Iran. A decline in joint gains or a shift in relative advantage away from the U.S. should incline the U.S., as the stronger party, to bring its superior strength to bear to adjust the rules of the game through bargaining tactics of issue linkage.

But here, once again, U.S. relations with Mexico, Japan, and Iran do not conform so neatly to expectations. Some use of issue linkage by the U.S. was observed with regard to all three of these states before the war, and just after the war with regard to Iran. But during and after the postwar global extension of U.S. foreign policy, tactics of cross-issue linkage were not in great evidence. Even the Nixon-Kissinger era, when "linkage" tactics in dealings with rival or adversary nations were fashionable, was not marked by heavy use of such tactics in dealings with the three allied nations considered in this study. In the case of Japan, the U.S. did link Okinawa reversion to Japanese concessions on textile trade. But this tactic—which proved a failure— remains the only conspicuous instance of a linkage policy employed by the U.S. in recent years in relations with Japan, Mexico, or Iran. It seems that habits of non-linkage can develop and endure even in the absence of complex interdependence, and even in the face of an advantage declining or shifting away from the stronger power.

In the case of U.S. relations with Japan, the linkage tactics of the Okinawa reversion era were not continued beyond that era. The U.S. import surcharge of 1971, although directed against the undervalued Japanese Yen, avoided any explicit or exclusive reference to Japan. And the Japanese decision to break with U.S. Middle East policy in response to the 1973 Arab oil embargo did not produce retaliatory "linkage," or even threats of linkage, from the U.S. Owing in part to the failure of the Okinawa linkage, and in part to the real adjustments which grew out of the "Nixon shocks" period, U.S. tactics of explicit issue linkage were thereafter discontinued.

In the case of Iran, strategies of issue linkage have been specifically rejected by the U.S. in recent years, despite Iran's push for higher OPEC oil prices. Suggestions that the U.S. might discontinue arms or food sales to Iran, pending some shift in Iranian oil policy, were cut short by top level pronouncements that differences over oil "should not stand in the way of cooperation in other areas to our mutual benefit."

Even in its recent relations with dependent Mexico, the U.S. government has not been tempted into a heavy-handed linkage strategy. As Mexican diplomacy moved steadily toward championing a new international economic order less favorable to the interests of the U.S., some sentiment formed for adopting a punitive response (such as denial of trade preferences should Mexico join the OPEC oil producer's alliance).[11] But neither the U.S. nor Mexico has yet forced this issue. The old regime of quiet diplomacy, tempered by Mexican dependence and U.S. distraction, persists.

So even where conditions of complex interdependence are not fully developed, and where conditions of "dependence" may add to the vulnerablility of the weak, and despite a shift in relative advantage away from the interests of the strong, tactics of issue-linkage toward Japan, Mexico, or Iran have not been freely employed. This habit of non-linkage may be attributed to several traditional phenomena. First is the simple calculation that linkage tactics against any one of these three nations will not work, and may only provide an unhappy precedent for later use of such tactics by other powers against the U.S. Second is the lingering notion that issue-linkage tactics are incompatible with the larger role of free world leadership which the U.S. still presumes to play. Issue-linkage may be one means of using strength, but it is considered at the same time to be a sign of declining strength. At the height of U.S. postwar expansion, maintenance of America's global position did not require such tactics. As long as the U.S. aspires to this leadership role, it will employ tactics of issue-linkage only with great reluctance.

In the longer run, this lingering leadership habit of non-linkage may not be sustainable. If the U.S. should weaken itself further by paying heavy leadership costs, or if the task of system maintenance should become more difficult as distant clients and allies become more assertive, or if the largest rewards of alliance fall more to others than to the U.S., then a more self-serving U.S. policy style might quickly reappear. Under these more desperate conditions, such a U.S. policy style would most likely provoke retaliation, and higher costs for all. A gradual transition away from unilateral U.S. leadership may be preferred to overburdened leadership leading to its rapid disappearance. The mutually advantageous character of recent U.S. relations with Japan, Mexico, and Iran, in the absence of fully developed complex interdependence, depends somewhat upon a U.S. habit of unilateral leadership. This habit produces a diplomatic style of self-restraint and leadership by inducement somewhat akin to that which grows from conditions of complex interdependence. But in the absence of full complex interdependence, it is a habit which may not endure.

NOTES

[1]This definition of dependence builds upon the distinction between sensitivity and vulnerability which Keohane and Nye develop, but which they do not incorporate into their ideal types of "realism" and "complex interdependence." Keohane and Nye concede that their argument might well be expanded to pay heed to the literature of "international dependence." See Keohane and Nye, *Power and Interdependence*, p. ix.

[2]Mexico is far from perfectly dependent upon the U.S., of course. U.S. relations with some even more peripheral Caribbean nation such as El Salvador or Guatemala would more nearly approximate ideal type "dependence."

[3]Keohane and Nye, *Power and Interdependence*, p. 175.

[4]*Ibid.*, p. 201

[5]It is of interest to note that even the Lockheed affair of 1976, which postdates this research, failed to provoke a high-level conflict between the U.S. and Japan. As Arthur W. Hummel, Jr., U.S. Assistant Secretary of State explained, "Despite its potential for doing so, the Lockheed affair had not significantly damaged U.S.-Japan relations. By treating the affair as a legal issue, and placing it solely within the purview of law enforcement agencies, the bilateral political relationship was successfully insulated." See U.S. Department of State Current Policy Release No. 15, October 1976.

[6]From the Keohane-Nye study, it is seen that even Australia found itself in frequent socio-economic conflict with the U.S. (eleven of twenty cases), despite a very low level of "complex interdependence." See *Power and Interdependence*, p. 200.

[7]For an extended review of U.S. foreign policy agenda content and dynamics, see Robert L. Paarlberg, "U.S. Attention to the Third World, 1945-74: The Logic of Foreign Policy Agenda Formation," Ph.D. dissertation, Department of Government, Harvard University, 1975.

[8]See Lawrence Olson, "Political Relations," in Herbert Passin, (ed.), *The United States and Japan* (Washington: Columbia Books, 1975), p. 64.

[9]Despite the insularity and dependence which burdened Mexico's postwar alliance relations with the U.S., it is of interest to note that the *least* favored of all object nations under consideration here was Australia. In sixteen postwar conflicts with the U.S., Australia managed to secure an outcome more favorable to its own objectives in only three cases. It seems that Australia could neither profit from the "complex interdependence" advantage of a Canada, from the strategic and industrial potential of a Japan, from Iran's ability to credibly threaten to "move toward non-alignment," nor even from the proximity or the attention advantage of a Mexico. Unlike Iran, Australia was closely tied to the West by the non-Asian character of its population, and by its unusual postwar sense of security vulnerablility. The government of Australia was one of few to believe, as *much* as the U.S., that Southeast Asian communist insurgents were indeed a first-order Cold War security threat. The strength of this belief placed Australia at some disadvantage in its dealings with the U.S. Iran, by contrast, moved sooner than the U.S. to recognize the limits of an international communist military threat in its own region of the world. Iranian security concerns dealt primarily with internal political opposition. So Iranian diplomats were able to maneuver within their U.S. security alliance with a sense of greater freedom, and to greater effect. For data on U.S.-Australia conflict see Keohane and Nye, *Power and Interdependence*, pp. 193-199.

[10]Keohane and Nye, *Power and Interdependence*, p. 214.

[11]At the non-governmental level, at least one punitive issue linkage strategy was employed against Mexico, when American Jewish organizations promoted a boycott on tourism to Mexico, hoping to reverse Mexico's support in the U.N. for a resolution equating Zionism with racism.

BOOKS WRITTEN UNDER CENTER AUSPICES

The Soviet Bloc, Zbigniew K. Brzezinski (sponsored jointly with the Russian Research Center), 1960. Harvard University Press. Revised edition 1967.

The Necessity for Choice, by Henry A. Kissinger, 1961. Harper & Bros.

Rift and Revolt in Hungary, by Ferenc A. Váli, 1961. Harvard University Press.

Strategy and Arms Control, by Thomas C. Schelling and Morton H. Halperin, 1961. Twentieth Century Fund.

United States Manufacturing Investment in Brazil, by Lincoln Gordon and Engelbert L. Grommers, 1962. Harvard Business School.

The Economy of Cyprus, by A.J. Meyer, with Simos Vassiliou (sponsored jointly with the Center for Middle Eastern Studies), 1962. Harvard University Press.

Entrepreneurs of Lebanon, by Yusif A. Sayigh (sponsored jointly with the Center for Middle Eastern Studies), 1962. Harvard University Press.

Communist China 1955-1959: Policy Documents with Analysis, with a foreward by Robert R. Bowie and John K. Fairbank (sponsored jointly with the East Asian Research Center), 1962. Harvard University Press.

Somali Nationalism, by Saadia Touval, 1963. Harvard University Press.

The Dilemma of Mexico's Development, by Raymond Vernon, 1963. Harvard University Press.

Limited War in the Nuclear Age, by Morton H. Halperin, 1963. John Wiley & Sons. (Reprinted 1978, Greenwood Press.)

In Search of France, by Stanley Hoffmann *et al.,* 1963. Harvard University Press.

The Arms Debate, by Robert A. Levine, 1963. Harvard University Press.

Africans on the Land, by Montague Yudelman, 1964. Harvard University Press.

Counterinsurgency Warfare, by David Galula, 1964. Frederick A. Praeger, Inc.

People and Policy in the Middle East, by Max Weston Thornburg, 1964. W.W. Norton & Co.

Shaping the Future, by Robert R. Bowie, 1964. Columbia University Press.

Foreign Aid and Foreign Policy, by Edward S. Mason (sponsored jointly with the Council on Foreign Relations), 1964. Harper & Row.

How Nations Negotiate, by Fred Charles Iklé, 1964. Harper & Row.

Public Policy and Private Enterprise in Mexico, edited by Raymond Vernon, 1964. Harvard University Press.

China and the Bomb, by Morton H. Halperin (sponsored jointly with the East Asian Research Center), 1965. Frederick A. Praeger, Inc.

Democracy in Germany, by Fritz Erler (Jodidi Lectures), 1965. Harvard University Press.

The Troubled Partnership, by Henry A. Kissinger (sponsored jointly with the Council on Foreign Relations), 1965. McGraw-Hill Book Co.

The Rise of Nationalism in Central Africa, by Robert I. Rotberg, 1965. Harvard University Press.

Pan-Africanism and East African Integration, by Joseph S. Nye, Jr., 1965. Harvard University Press.

Communist China and Arms Control, by Morton H. Halperin and Dwight H. Perkins (sponsored jointly with the East Asian Research Center), 1965. Frederick A. Praeger, Inc.

Problems of National Strategy, ed. Henry Kissinger, 1965. Frederick A. Praeger, Inc.

Deterrence before Hiroshima: The Airpower Background of Modern Strategy, by George H. Quester, 1966. John Wiley & Sons.

Containing the Arms Race, by Jeremy J. Stone, 1966. M.I.T. Press.

Germany and the Atlantic Alliance: The Interaction of Strategy and Politics, by James L. Richardson, 1966. Harvard University Press.

Arms and Influence, by Thomas C. Schelling, 1966. Yale University Press.

Political Change in a West African State, by Martin Kilson, 1966. Harvard University Press.

Planning Without Facts: Lessons in Resource Allocation from Nigeria's Development, by Wolfgang F. Stolper, 1966. Harvard University Press.

Export Instability and Economic Development, by Alasdair I. MacBean, 1966. Harvard University Press.

Foreign Policy and Democratic Politics, by Kenneth N. Waltz (sponsored jointly with the Institute of War and Peace Studies, Columbia University), 1967, Little, Brown & Co.

Contemporary Military Strategy, by Morton H. Halperin, 1967. Little, Brown & Co.

Sino-Soviet Relations and Arms Control, ed. Morton H. Halperin (sponsored jointly with the East Asian Research Center), 1967. M.I.T. Press.

Africa and United States Policy, by Rupert Emerson, 1967. Prentice-Hall.

Elites in Latin America, edited by Seymour M. Lipset and Aldo Solari, 1967. Oxford University Press.

Europe's Postwar Growth, by Charles P. Kindleberger, 1967. Harvard University Press.

The Rise and Decline of the Cold War, by Paul Seabury, 1967. Basic Books.

Student Politics, ed. S.M. Lipset, 1967. Basic Books.

Pakistan's Development: Social Goals and Private Incentives, by Gustav F. Papenek, 1967. Harvard University Press.

Strike a Blow and Die: A Narrative of Race Relations in Colonial Africa, by George Simeon Mwase, ed. Robert I. Rotberg, 1967. Harvard University Press.

Party Systems and Voter Alignments, edited by Seymour M. Lipset and

Stein Rokkan, 1967. Free Press.

Agrarian Socialism, by Seymour M. Lipset, revised edition, 1968. Doubleday Anchor.

Aid, Influence, and Foreign Policy, by Joan M. Nelson, 1968. The Macmillan Company.

Development Policy: Theory and Practice, edited by Gustav F. Papanek, 1968. Harvard University Press.

International Regionalism, by Joseph S. Nye. 1968. Little, Brown & Co.

Revolution and Counterrevolution, by Seymour M. Lipset, 1968. Basic Books.

Political Order in Changing Societies, by Samuel P. Huntington, 1968. Yale University Press.

The TFX Decision: McNamara and the Military, by Robert J. Art, 1968. Little, Brown & Co.

Korea: The Politics of the Vortex, by Gregory Henderson, 1968. Harvard University Press.

Political Development in Latin America, by Martin Needler, 1968. Random House.

The Precarious Republic, by Michael Hudson, 1968. Random House.

The Brazilian Capital Goods Industry, 1929-1964 (sponsored jointly with the Center for Studies in Education and Development), by Nathaniel H. Leff, 1968. Harvard University Press.

Economic Policy-Making and Development in Brazil, 1947-1964, by Nathaniel H. Leff, 1968. John Wiley & Sons.

Turmoil and Transition: Higher Education and Student Politics in India, edited by Philip G. Altbach, 1968. Lalvani Publishing House (Bombay).

German Foreign Policy in Transition, by Karl Kaiser, 1968. Oxford University Press.

Protest and Power in Black Africa, edited by Robert I. Rotberg, 1969 Oxford University Press.

Peace in Europe, by Karl E. Birnbaum, 1969. Oxford University Press.

The Process of Modernization: An Annotated Bibliography on the Socio-cultural Aspects of Development, by John Brode, 1969. Harvard University Press.

Students in Revolt, edited by Seymour M. Lipset and Philip G. Altbach, 1969. Houghton Mifflin.

Agricultural Development in India's Districts: The Intensive Agricultural Districts Programme, by Dorris D. Brown, 1970. Harvard University Press.

Authoritarian Politics in Modern Society: The Dynamics of Established One-Party Systems, edited by Samuel P. Huntington and Clement H. Moore, 1970. Basic Books.

Nuclear Diplomacy, by George H. Quester, 1970. Dunellen.

The Logic of Images in International Relations, by Robert Jervis, 1970. Princeton University Press.

Europe's Would-Be Polity, by Leon Lindberg and Stuart A. Scheingold, 1970. Prentice-Hall.

Taxation and Development: Lessons from Colombian Experience, by Richard M. Bird, 1970. Harvard University Press.

Lord and Peasant in Peru: A Paradigm of Political and Social Change, by F. LaMond Tullis, 1970. Harvard University Press.

The Kennedy Round in American Trade Policy: The Twilight of the GATT? by John W. Evans, 1971. Harvard University Press.

Korean Development: The Interplay of Politics and Economics, by David C. Cole and Princeton N. Lyman, 1971. Harvard University Press.

Development Policy II—The Pakistan Experience, edited by Walter P. Falcon and Gustav F. Papanek, 1971. Harvard University Press.

Higher Education in a Transitional Society, by Philip G. Altbach, 1971. Sindhu Publications (Bombay).

Studies in Development Planning, edited by Hollis B. Chenery, 1971. Harvard University Press.

Passion and Politics, by Seymour M. Lipset with Gerald Schaflander, 1971. Little, Brown & Co.

Political Mobilization of the Venezuelan Peasant, by John D. Powell, 1971. Harvard University Press.

Higher Education in India, edited by Amrik Singh and Philip Altbach, 1971. Oxford University Press (Delhi).

The Myth of the Guerrilla, by J. Bowyer Bell, 1971. Blond (London) and Knopf (New York).

International Norms and War between States: Three Studies in International Politics, by Kjell Goldmann, 1971. Published jointly by Läromedelsförlagen (Sweden) and the Swedish Institute of International Affairs.

Peace in Parts: Integration and Conflict in Regional Organization, by Joseph S. Nye, Jr., 1971. Little, Brown & Co.

Sovereignty at Bay: The Multinational Spread of U.S. Enterprise,, by Raymond Vernon, 1971. Basic Books.

Defense Strategy for the Seventies (revision of *Contemporary Military Strategy*) by Morton H. Halperin, 1971. Little, Brown & Co.

Peasants Against Politics: Rural Organization in Brittany, 1911-1967, by Suzanne Berger, 1972. Harvard University Press.

Transnational Relations and World Politics, edited by Robert O. Keohane and Joseph S. Nye, Jr., 1972. Harvard University Press.

Latin American University Students: A Six-Nation Study, by Arthur Liebman, Kenneth N. Walker, and Myron Glazer, 1972. Harvard University Press.

The Politics of Land Reform in Chile, 1950-1970: Public Policy, Political Institutions and Social Change, by Robert R. Kaufman, 1972. Harvard University Press.

The Boundary Politics of Independent Africa, by Saadia Touval, 1972.

Harvard University Press.

The Politics of Nonviolent Action, by Gene E. Sharp, 1973. Porter Sargent.

System 37 Viggen: Arms, Technology, and the Domestication of Glory, by Ingemar Dörfer, 1973. Universitets forlaget (Oslo).

University Students and African Politics, by William John Hanna, 1974. Africana Publishing Company.

Organizing the Transnational: The Experience with Transnational Enterprise in Advanced Technology, by M.S. Hochmuth, 1974. Sijthoff (Leiden).

Becoming Modern, by Alex Inkeles and David H. Smith, 1974. Harvard University Press.

The United States and West Germany 1945-1973: A Study in Alliance Politics, by Roger Morgan (sponsored jointly with the Royal Institute of International Affairs), 1974. Oxford University Press.

Multinational Corporations and the Politics of Dependence: Copper in Chile, 1945-1973, by Theodore Moran, 1974. Princeton University Press.

The Andean Group: A Case Study in Economic Integration Among Developing Countries, by David Morawetz, 1974. M.I.T. Press.

Kenya: The Politics of Participation and Control, by Henry Bienen, 1974. Princeton University Press.

Land Reform and Politics: A Comparative Analysis, by Hung-chao Tai, 1974. University of California Press.

Big Business and the State: Changing Relations in Western Europe, edited by Raymond Vernon, 1974. Harvard University Press.

Economic Policymaking in a Conflict Society: The Argentine Case, by Richard D. Mallon and Juan V. Sourrouille, 1975. Harvard University Press.

New States in the Modern World, edited by Martin Kilson, 1975. Harvard University Press.

Revolutionary Civil War: The Elements of Victory and Defeat, by David Wilkinson, 1975. Page-Ficklin Publications.

Politics and the Migrant Poor in Mexico City, by Wayne A. Cornelius, 1975. Stanford University Press.

East Africa and the Orient: Cultural Syntheses in Pre-Colonial Times, ed. H. Neville Chittick and Robert I. Rotberg, 1975. Africana Publishing Company.

No Easy Choice: Political Participation in Developing Countries, by Samuel P. Huntington and Joan M. Nelson, 1976. Harvard University Press.

The Politics of International Monetary Reform—The Exchange Crisis, by Michael J. Brenner, 1976. Ballinger Publishing Co.

The International Politics of Natural Resources, by Zuhayr Mikdashi, 1976. Cornell University Press.

The Oil Crisis, edited by Raymond Vernon, 1976. W.W. Norton & Co.

Social Change and Political Participation in Turkey, by Ergun Ozbudun, 1976. Princeton University Press.

The Arabs, Israelis, and Kissinger: A Secret History of American Diplomacy in the Middle East, by Edward R.F. Sheehan, 1976. Reader's Digest Press.

Perception and Misperception in International Politics, by Robert Jervis, 1976. Princeton University Press.

Power and Interdependence, by Robert O. Keohane and Joseph S. Nye, Jr., 1977. Little, Brown.

Soldiers in Politics: Military Coups and Governments, by Eric Nordlinger, 1977. Prentice-Hall.

The Military and Politics in Modern Times: On Professionals, Praetorians, and Revolutionary Soldiers, by Amos Perlmutter, 1977. Yale University Press.

Money and Power: Banks and the World Monetary System, by Jonathan David Aronson, 1977. Sage Publications.

Bankers and Borders: The Case of the American Banks in Britain, by Janet Kelly, 1977. Ballinger Publishing Co.

Shattered Peace: The Origins of the Cold War and the National Security State, by Daniel Yergin, 1977. Houghton Mifflin.

Storm Over the Multinationals: The Real Issues, by Raymond Vernon, 1977. Harvard University Press.

Political Generations and Political Development, ed. Richard J. Samuels, 1977. Lexington Books.

Cuba: Order and Revolution, by Jorge I. Dominguez, 1978. Harvard University Press.

Defending the National Interest: Raw Materials Investments and American Foreign Policy, by Stephen D. Krasner, 1978. Princeton University Press.

Commodity Conflict: The Political Economy of International Commodity Negotiations, by L.N. Rangarajan, 1978. Cornell University Press and Croom Helm (London).

Standing Guard: The Protection of Foreign Investment, by Charles Lipson, 1978. University of California Press.

Israel: Embattled Ally, by Nadav Safran, 1978. Harvard University Press.

Access to Power: Political Participation by the Urban Poor in Developing Nations, by Joan M. Nelson, 1979. Princeton University Press.

HARVARD STUDIES IN INTERNATIONAL AFFAIRS*

(Formerly Occasional Papers in International Affairs).

*Available from Harvard University Center for International Affairs, 1737 Cambridge St. Cambridge, Massachusetts 02138

†Out of print. Reprints may be ordered from AMS Press, Inc., 56 East 13th Street, New York, N.Y. 10003

†20. *East and West Pakistan: A Problem in the Political Economy of Regional Planning*, by Md. Anisur Rahman, 1968.

†21. *Internal War and International Systems: Perspectives on Method*, by George A. Kelley and Linda B. Miller, 1969.

†22. *Migrants, Urban Poverty, and Instability in Developing Nations*, by Joan M. Nelson, 1969. 81 pp.

23. *Growth and Development in Pakistan, 1955-1969*, by Joseph J. Stern and Walter P. Falcon, 1970. 94 pp. $3.50.

24. *Higher Education in Developing Countries: A Select Bibliography*, by Philip G. Altbach, 1970. 118 pp. $4.50.

25. *Anatomy of Political Institutionalization: The Case of Israel and Some Comparative Analyses*, by Amos Perlmutter, 1970. 60 pp. $2.95.

†26. *The German Democratic Republic from the Sixties to the Seventies*, by Peter Christian Ludz, 1970. 100 pp.

27. *The Law in Political Integration: The Evolution and Integrative Implications of Regional Legal Processes in the European Community*, by Stuart A. Scheingold, 1971. 63 pp. $2.95.

29. *Conflict Regulation in Divided Societies*, by Eric A. Nordlinger, 1972. 142 pp. $4.95.

30. *Israel's Political-Military Doctrine*, by Michael I. Handel, 1973. 101 pp. $3.75.

31. *Italy, NATO, and the European Community: The Interplay of Foreign Policy and Domestic Politics*, by Primo Vannicelli, 1974. 67 + x pp. $3.75.

32. *The Choice of Technology in Developing Countries: Some Cautionary Tales*, by C. Peter Timmer, John W. Thomas, Louis T. Wells. Jr., and David Morawetz, 1975. 114 pp. $3.95.

33. *The International Role of the Communist Parties of Italy and France*, by Donald L.M. Blackmer and Annie Kriegel, 1975. 67 + x pp. $3.50.

34. *The Hazards of Peace: A European View of Detente*, by Juan Cassiers, 1976. 94 pp. $3.50.

35. *Oil and the Middle East War: Europe in the Energy Crisis*, by Robert J. Lieber, 1976. 75 + x pp. $3.45.

37. *Climatic Change and World Affairs*, by Crispin Tickell, 1977. 78 pp. $3.95.

38. *Conflict and Violence in Lebanon: Confrontation in the Middle East*, by Walid Khalidi, 1979. Ca. 170 pp. $12.95, cloth; $6.95, paper.

39. *Diplomatic Dispute: U.S. Conflict with Iran, Japan, and Mexico*, by Robert L. Paarlberg, ed., Eul. Y. Park, and Donald L. Wyman, 1979. 173 pp. $11.95, cloth; $5.95, paper.

40. *Commandos and Politicians: Elite Military Units in Modern Democracies*, by Eliot A. Cohen, 1978. 136 pp. $8.95, cloth; $3.95, paper.

41. *Yellow Earth, Green Jade: Constants in Chinese Political Mores,* by Simon de Beaufort, 1979. Ca. 90 pp. $8.95, cloth; $3.95, paper.
42. *The Future of North America: Canada, The United States, and Quebec Nationalism,* edited by Elliot J. Feldman and Neil Nevitte, 1979. Ca. 378 pp. $13.95, cloth; $6.95, paper.